INS 22 Course Guide

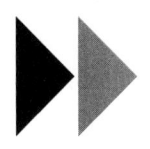

Personal Insurance
5th Edition

American Institute for Chartered Property Casualty Underwriters/Insurance Institute of America

720 Providence Road • Suite 100 • Malvern, PA 19355-3433

© 2008

American Institute for Chartered Property Casualty Underwriters/Insurance Institute of America

All rights reserved. This book or any part thereof may not be reproduced without the written permission of the copyright holder.

Unless otherwise apparent, examples used in AICPCU/IIA materials related to this course are based on hypothetical situations and are for educational purposes only. The characters, persons, products, services, and organizations described in these examples are fictional. Any similarity or resemblance to any other character, person, product, services, or organization is merely coincidental. AICPCU/IIA is not responsible for such coincidental or accidental resemblances.

This material may contain Internet Web site links external to AICPCU/IIA. AICPCU/IIA neither approves nor endorses any information, products, or services to which any external Web sites refer. Nor does AICPCU/IIA control these Web sites' content or the procedures for Web site content development.

AICPCU/IIA specifically disclaims any implied warranties of merchantability or fitness for a particular purpose. No warranty may be created or extended by sales representatives or written sales materials.

AICPCU/IIA materials related to this course are provided with the understanding that AICPCU/IIA is not engaged in rendering legal, accounting, or other professional service. Nor is AICPCU/IIA explicitly or implicitly stating that any of the processes, procedures, or policies described in the materials are the only appropriate ones to use. The advice and strategies contained herein may not be suitable for every situation.

Information which is copyrighted by and proprietary to Insurance Services Office, Inc. ("ISO Material") is included in this publication. Use of the ISO Material is limited to ISO Participating Insurers and their Authorized Representatives. Use by ISO Participating Insurers is limited to use in those jurisdictions for which the insurer has an appropriate participation with ISO. Use of the ISO Material by Authorized Representatives is limited to use solely on behalf of one or more ISO Participating Insurers.

This publication includes forms which are provided for review purposes only. These forms may not be used, in whole or in part, by any company or individuals not licensed by Insurance Services Office, Inc. (ISO) for the applicable line of insurance and jurisdiction to which this form applies. It is a copyright infringement to include any part(s) of this form within independent company programs without the written permission of ISO.

Fifth Edition • Second Printing • May 2009

ISBN 978-0-89463-364-5

Contents

Study Materials iii
Student Resources iv
Using This Course Guide iv

Assignments

1. Personal Insurance Overview 1.1
2. Automobile Insurance and Society 2.1
3. Personal Auto Policy: Liability, Medical Payments, and Uninsured Motorists Coverage 3.1
4. Personal Auto Policy: Physical Damage, Duties After an Accident, Endorsements, and General Provisions 4.1
5. Homeowners Property Coverage 5.1
6. Homeowners Liability Coverage 6.1
7. Homeowners Coverage Forms and Endorsements 7.1
8. Other Residential Insurance 8.1
9. Other Personal Property and Liability Insurance 9.1
10. Personal Loss Exposures and Financial Planning 10.1
11. Life Insurance 11.1
12. Health and Disability Insurance 12.1

Study Materials Available for INS 22

Personal Insurance, 2nd ed., 2008, AICPCU/IIA.

INS 22 *Course Guide,* 5th ed., 2008, AICPCU/IIA (includes access code for SMART Online Practice Exams).

INS 22 SMART Study Aids—Review Notes and Flash Cards, 3rd ed.

Student Resources

Catalog A complete listing of our offerings can be found in *Succeed*, the Institutes' professional development catalog, including information about:

- Current programs and courses
- Current textbooks, course guides, and SMART Study Aids
- Program completion requirements
- Exam registration

To obtain a copy of the catalog, visit our Web site at www.aicpcu.org or contact Customer Service at (800) 644-2101.

How To Pass Institute Exams! This free handbook, printable from the Student Services Center on the Institutes' Web site at www.aicpcu.org, or available by calling Customer Service at (800) 644-2101, is designed to help you by:

- Giving you ideas on how to use textbooks and course guides as effective learning tools
- Providing steps for answering exam questions effectively
- Recommending exam-day strategies

Institutes Online Forums Do you wish you could talk with people around the country about course questions and share information with others who have similar professional interests? We host forums at our Web site, where you can do just that. To access our forums:

- Go to the Institutes' Web site at www.aicpcu.org
- Click on the "Log on. Learn." link
- Scroll down and click on "Forums"
- Read the instructions, and you're ready to go!

Educational Services To ensure that you take courses matching both your needs and your skills, you can obtain advice from the Institutes by:

- E-mailing your questions to advising@cpcuiia.org
- Calling an Institutes' advisor directly at (610) 644-2100, ext. 7601
- Obtaining, completing, and submitting a self-inventory form, available on our Web site at www.aicpcu.org or by contacting Customer Service at (800) 644-2101

Exam Registration Information As you proceed with your studies, be sure to arrange for your exam.

- Consult the registration booklet that accompanied this course guide for complete information regarding exam dates and fees worldwide. Plan to register with the Institutes well in advance of your exam to take advantage of any discounted rates.
- If your registration booklet does not include exam dates for the current year, you can obtain up-to-date exam information by visiting the Institutes' Web site at www.aicpcu.org, sending an e-mail to customerservice@cpcuiia.org, or calling the Institutes at (800) 644-2101.

How to Contact the Institutes For more information on any of these publications and services:

- Visit our Web site at www.aicpcu.org
- Telephone us at (800) 644-2101 or (610) 644-2100 outside the U.S.
- E-mail us at customerservice@cpcuiia.org
- Fax us at (610) 640-9576
- Write us at AICPCU/IIA, Customer Service, 720 Providence Road, Suite 100, Malvern, PA 19355-3433

Using This Course Guide

This course guide will help you learn the course content and pass the exam.

Each assignment in this course guide typically includes the following components:

Educational Objectives These are the most important study tools in the course guide. Because all of the questions on the exam are based on the Educational Objectives, the best way to study for the exam is to focus on these objectives.

Each Educational Objective typically begins with one of the following action words, which indicate the level of understanding required for the exam:

Analyze—Determine the nature and the relationship of the parts.

Apply—Put to use for a practical purpose.

Calculate—Determine numeric values by mathematical process.

Classify—Arrange or organize according to class or category.

Compare—Show similarities and differences.

Contrast—Show only differences.

Define—Give a clear, concise meaning.

Describe—Represent or give an account.

Evaluate—Determine the value or merit.

Explain—Relate the importance or application.

Identify or list—Name or make a list.

Illustrate—Give an example.

Justify—Show to be right or reasonable.

Paraphrase—Restate in your own words.

Summarize—Concisely state the main points.

Required Reading The items listed in this section indicate what portion of the study materials (the textbook chapter(s), course guide readings, or other assigned materials) correspond to the assignment.

Outline The outline lists the topics in the assignment. Read the outline before the required reading to become familiar with the assignment content and the relationships of topics.

Key Words and Phrases These words and phrases are fundamental to understanding the assignment and have a common meaning for those working in insurance. After completing the required reading, test your understanding of the assignment's key words and phrases by writing their definitions.

For help, refer to the page numbers that appear in parentheses after each key word and phrase.

Review Questions The review questions test your understanding of what you have read. Review the Educational Objectives and required reading, then answer the questions to the best of your ability. When you are finished, check the answers at the end of the assignment to evaluate your comprehension.

Application Questions These questions continue to test your knowledge of the required reading by applying what you've studied to real-life situations. Again, check the suggested answers at the end of the assignment to review your progress.

Sample Exam The sample exam helps you test your knowledge of the material. Use the sample exam at the back of the course guide or the SMART Online Practice Exams to become familiar with the test format. A printable sample national exam is included as part of the SMART Online Practice Exams product. Once you have activated the course using the access code found on the inside back cover of this course guide, you can download and print a sample national exam. The Online Practice Exams product also allows you to take full practice exams using the same software that you will use when you take your national exam.

More Study Aids

The Institutes also produce supplemental study tools, called SMART Study Aids, for many of their courses. When SMART Study Aids are available for a course, they are listed on both page iii of this course guide and on the first page of each assignment. SMART Study Aids include review notes and flash cards and are excellent tools to help you learn and retain the information contained in each assignment.

SEGMENT A

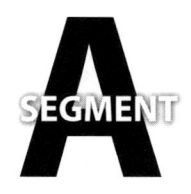

Assignment 1　　Personal Insurance Overview

Assignment 2　　Automobile Insurance and Society

Assignment 3　　Personal Auto Policy: Liability, Medical Payments, and Uninsured Motorists Coverage

Assignment 4　　Personal Auto Policy: Physical Damage, Duties After an Accident, Endorsements, and General Provisions

Segment A is the first of three segments in the INS 22 course. These segments are designed to help structure your study.

Direct Your Learning

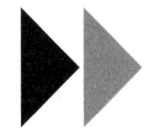

ASSIGNMENT 1

Personal Insurance Overview

Educational Objectives

After learning the content of this assignment, you should be able to:

1. Summarize the three elements of loss exposures.

2. Describe the property loss exposures that individuals and families might face in terms of each of the following:
   - The assets exposed to loss
   - The causes of loss
   - The financial consequences of loss

3. Describe the liability loss exposures that individuals and families might face in terms of each of the following:
   - The assets exposed to loss
   - The causes of loss
   - The financial consequences of loss

4. Describe the personal financial planning loss exposures that individuals and families might face in terms of each of the following:
   - The assets exposed to loss
   - The causes of loss
   - The financial consequences of loss

5. Summarize the six steps of the risk management process.

6. Identify the risk control and risk financing techniques used by individuals and families.

7. Explain how personal insurance is used as a risk management technique.

8. Summarize the contents of the six common categories of policy provisions of a property-casualty insurance policy.

9. Describe the primary methods of insurance policy analysis.

Study Materials

Required Reading:
▶ Personal Insurance
  - Chapter 1

Study Aids:
▶ SMART Online Practice Exams
▶ SMART Study Aids
  - Review Notes and Flash Cards—Assignment 1

Outline

- **Elements of Loss Exposures**
  A. Asset Exposed to Loss
  B. Cause of Loss
  C. Financial Consequences of Loss
- **Property Loss Exposures**
  A. Assets Exposed to Loss
    1. Real Property
    2. Personal Property
  B. Causes of Loss
  C. Financial Consequences of Loss
- **Liability Loss Exposures**
  A. Assets Exposed to Loss
  B. Causes of Loss
    1. Tort Liability
    2. Contractual Liability
    3. Statutory Liability
  C. Financial Consequences of Loss
- **Personal Financial Planning Loss Exposures**
  A. Retirement Loss Exposures
  B. Premature Death Loss Exposures
  C. Health and Disability Loss Exposures
  D. Unemployment
- **Risk Management Process**
  A. Step 1: Identifying Loss Exposures
  B. Step 2: Analyzing Loss Exposures
  C. Step 3: Examining the Feasibility of Risk Management Techniques
  D. Step 4: Selecting the Appropriate Risk Management Techniques
  E. Step 5: Implementing the Selected Risk Management Techniques
  F. Step 6: Monitoring Results and Revising the Risk Management Program
- **Risk Management Techniques**
  A. Risk Control Techniques
    1. Avoidance
    2. Loss Prevention
    3. Loss Reduction
    4. Separation
    5. Duplication
    6. Diversification
  B. Risk Financing Techniques
    1. Retention
    2. Transfer
  C. Insurance for Property and Liability Loss Exposures
  D. Retirement Loss Exposures
  E. Premature Death Loss Exposures
  F. Health and Disability Loss Exposures
  G. Unemployment Loss Exposures
- **Common Policy Provisions**
  A. Declarations
  B. Definitions
  C. Insuring Agreements
  D. Conditions
  E. Exclusions
  F. Miscellaneous Provisions
- **Policy Analysis**
  A. Pre-Loss Policy Analysis
  B. Post-Loss Policy Analysis
- **Summary**

study tips — If you are not sure that you have the current edition of the textbook(s), course guide, or registration booklet for the exam you plan to take, please contact the Institutes (see page iv).

Personal Insurance Overview 1.3

For each assignment, you should define or describe each of the Key Words and Phrases and answer each of the Review and Application Questions.

Educational Objective 1
Summarize the three elements of loss exposures.

Key Words and Phrases

Loss exposure

Cause of loss

Review Questions

1-1. What is an asset exposed to loss?

1-2. What is a cause of loss?

1-3. The financial consequences of loss are dependent on what factors?

Application Question

1-4. Joe has just purchased a new home. Assess whether all the necessary elements of a loss exposure are present.

Educational Objective 2
Describe the property loss exposures that individuals and families might face in terms of each of the following:
- The assets exposed to loss
- The causes of loss
- The financial consequences of loss

Key Words and Phrases
Property loss exposure

Real property

Personal property

Review Questions

2-1. What is a property loss exposure?

2-2. Individuals and families may own assets that are exposed to loss. Assets are any items of property that have value.

   a. What are two types of property that individuals and families own that may be exposed to loss?

   b. For your answers to (a), provide an example for each.

2-3. Name some causes of loss that might damage or destroy a dwelling.

2-4. What are three financial consequences of loss?

Application Question

2-5. Virtually all individuals and families have property loss exposures. Assume a family owns a fully furnished home that includes a yard, storage shed, and several fruit trees.

   a. What are the assets exposed to loss that the family might have as a consequence of home ownership?

   b. What are the causes of loss the family might face as a consequence of home ownership?

   c. What are the financial consequences of loss the family might face arising from home ownership?

Educational Objective 3

Describe the liability loss exposures that individuals and families might face in terms of each of the following:
- The assets exposed to loss
- The causes of loss
- The financial consequences of loss

Key Words and Phrases

Liability loss exposure

Damages

General damages

Special damages

Punitive, or exemplary, damages

Civil law

Tort

Negligence

Review Questions

3-1. Identify the assets exposed to loss in a liability loss exposure.

3-2. Identify the cause of loss associated with a liability loss exposure.

3-3. Describe the financial consequences of a liability loss exposure.

3-4. Identify the four elements of negligence.

3-5. Identify four examples of intentional torts.

Application Question

3-6. Sean has a disagreement with his neighbor, John, and physically harms him, causing John to be admitted to the hospital. John subsequently files a lawsuit against Sean.

a. Which of Sean's assets are exposed to loss?

b. What is the cause of Sean's loss?

c. What are the potential financial consequences for Sean?

Educational Objective 4

Describe the personal financial planning loss exposures that individuals and families might face in terms of each of the following:

- The assets exposed to loss
- The causes of loss
- The financial consequences of loss

Key Words and Phrases

Personal financial planning loss exposures

Temporary partial disability

Temporary total disability

Permanent partial disability

Permanent total disability

Review Questions

4-1. Identify the assets exposed to loss when an individual retires.

4-2. Describe the causes of loss associated with health and disability loss exposures.

4-3. Identify the four types of disability classifications.

Application Question

4-4. Assume Anton, a husband and father, dies prematurely.

a. What are the assets exposed to loss as a result of his death?

b. What is the financial cause of loss?

Educational Objective 5
Summarize the six steps of the risk management process.

Key Words and Phrases
Risk management process

Risk control

Risk financing

Review Questions

5-1. List the six steps of the risk management process.

5-2. Describe the loss characteristics that individuals and families may use to analyze their loss exposures.

5-3. Describe an example of measures that individuals and families might use to implement the selected risk management techniques.

Application Question

5-4. A family plans to analyze its automobile loss exposures. The mother and father each drive an older-model car. Their three daughters live with them and regularly use their cars in the evenings. Over the last three years, the family has been involved in four minor auto accidents. How might the family use the four dimensions of a loss exposure to analyze its automobile loss exposures?

Educational Objective 6
Identify the risk control and risk financing techniques used by individuals and families.

Key Words and Phrases

Avoidance

Loss prevention

Loss reduction

Separation

Duplication

Diversification

Retention

Deductible

Insurance

Transfer

Review Questions

6-1. Identify the risk control techniques used by individuals and families.

6-2. Identify the risk financing techniques used by individuals and families.

6-3. Describe two noninsurance risk transfer techniques.

6-4. Compare loss prevention to loss reduction.

6-5. Contrast planned retention and unplanned retention.

Application Question

6-6. For each of these sets of frequency-severity characteristics, explain whether you would retain or transfer a personal loss exposure with those characteristics:

   a. Low severity and low frequency

   b. High severity and low frequency

   c. Low severity and high frequency

   d. Medium severity and medium frequency

Educational Objective 7
Explain how personal insurance is used as a risk management technique.

Key Word or Phrase
Workers compensation

Review Questions

7-1. Identify the risk financing techniques individuals and families use to manage their loss exposures.

7-2. Identify the three layers of personal insurance.

7-3. Contrast the sources of property and liability loss exposures.

7-4. Identify examples of retirement loss exposures.

7-5. Describe how individuals and families can mitigate the financial consequences of retirement loss exposures.

7-6. Identify an example of a premature death loss exposure.

7-7. Contrast the needs-based approach and the human life value approaches used to determine the amount of insurance that an individual or family should purchase.

7-8. Why may health and disability insurance be more important to an individual or family than life insurance?

Personal Insurance Overview   1.19

7-9. Under what circumstances would a state extend the period over which unemployed individuals can receive benefits?

Application Question

7-10. Jerry and Linda are 45 and 42 years of age, respectively. They have three children, ages 18, 15, and 12. Jerry is employed full-time. Identify the types of insurance that the family should consider to manage the risks it faces.

Educational Objective 8
Summarize the contents of the six common categories of policy provisions of a property-casualty insurance policy.

Key Words and Phrases
Policy provision

Declarations

Endorsement

Definitions

Insuring agreement

Policy conditions

Exclusions

Review Questions

8-1. Summarize the contents of a property-casualty insurance policy's declarations.

8-2. Describe the interpretation rules a policy applies to undefined words and phrases.

8-3. Summarize the contents of a property-casualty insurance policy's insuring agreement.

Application Question

8-4. Paul, a policy analyst, needs to know the effect on coverage of each of the insurance policy provision categories. Paul's boss, Rachel, asks you to create a chart to assist Paul in learning the effect of each of the policy provision categories. What would you include in the chart to note the effect on coverage of each of the policy provision categories?

Educational Objective 9
Describe the primary methods of insurance policy analysis.

Review Questions

9-1. Describe the sources of information insureds may use to generate scenarios for pre-loss policy analysis.

9-2. Describe a limitation of scenario analysis.

9-3. Describe the primary method of post-loss policy analysis.

Application Question

9-4. A family's home is destroyed by a fire. Explain how a claims adjuster for the home's insurer could determine whether the loss was covered by the family's homeowners policy.

Answers to Assignment 1 Questions

NOTE: These answers are provided to give students a basic understanding of acceptable types of responses. They often are not the only valid answers and are not intended to provide an exhaustive response to the questions.

Educational Objective 1

1-1. An asset exposed to loss can be any item with value that is exposed to a possible reduction in value due to loss.

1-2. A cause of loss (or peril) is the means by which an asset can be reduced in value.

1-3. The financial consequences of loss are dependent on these factors:
- Type of asset exposed to loss
- Cause of loss
- Severity of loss

1-4. All the elements of a loss exposure are present for Joe:
- Asset exposed to loss—Joe's new home.
- Cause of loss—The possibility that a loss (a reduction in value to the asset) could occur to the new home
- Financial consequences—If a loss occurs, it generates financial consequences for Joe.

Educational Objective 2

2-1. A property loss exposure is any condition or situation that presents the possibility of a property loss.

2-2. a. Two types of property that individuals and families own that may be exposed to loss are (1) real property and (2) personal property.
  b. (1) Examples of real property that may be exposed to loss can include a home, foundations, underground pipes, sheds attached to the land, or anything growing on the land, including trees. (Other real property examples are acceptable.)

  (2) Examples of personal property that may be exposed to loss can include furniture; televisions; electronic equipment, including computers; and additional household personal property, such as appliances, dishes, carpets, sports equipment, clothing, tools, books, jewelry, cameras, and digital recording devices. Other examples of personal property that may be exposed to loss can include autos, boats, and intangible property. (Other personal property examples are acceptable.)

2-3. Causes of loss (or perils) that can damage or destroy real property, such as a dwelling, include fire, lightning, earthquake, or wind. (Other real property/dwelling cause of loss examples are acceptable.)

2-4. Financial consequences of loss can include one or more of these outcomes:
- Reduction in value of property—the difference between the value of the property before the loss (preloss value) and after the loss (post-loss value).
- Increased expenses—expenses in addition to normal living expenses that are necessary because of the loss.
- Lost income—loss of income that results if property is damaged.

2-5. a. Assets exposed to loss include real property and personal property. Real property can include the family's home, foundation, any underground pipes, the storage shed, the land, and the fruit trees. Personal property is all property other than real property, including all the furnishings (or contents) of the home. Such household furnishings for the family might include furniture, carpets, electronics, dishware, clothing, appliances, and numerous other items (accept other real property and personal property examples).

b. Causes of loss damage or destroy both real and personal property. As a consequence of home ownership, the family might face such causes of loss affecting their dwelling and furnishings as fire, lightning, earthquake, or wind (accept other causes of loss examples).

c. Financial consequences of loss the family might face arising from home ownership include one or more of these outcomes:
- Reduction in value to the home and furnishings—If a loss occurs, the value of the home and its contents may be worth less after the loss than they were worth before the loss.
- Increased expenses—If a loss occurs to the home and its furnishings, the family may face increased living expenses (such as the cost of hotel room rental) in addition to normal living expenses.
- Lost income—If a loss occurs, in some instances, the family may suffer loss of income as a result of the property damage.

Educational Objective 3

3-1. The assets exposed to loss in a liability loss exposure are money or other financial assets.

3-2. The cause of loss associated with a liability loss exposure is the claim of liability or the filing of a lawsuit.

3-3. The financial consequences of a liability loss exposure are that an individual or family may lose money or other financial assets. For example, they may have to pay to investigate and defend against the liability claim. Also, a court may award monetary damages if the defense of the claim is not successful or if the claim is settled out of court.

3-4. These are the four elements of negligence:
- A duty to act.
- A breach of that duty.
- An injury or damage occurs.
- The breach of duty is a direct cause of the injury or damage in an unbroken chain of events.

3-5. These are examples of intentional torts:
- Libel
- Slander
- Assault
- Battery
- Trespass
- Nuisance

3-6. a. The assets exposed to loss are Sean's money and other financial assets.
  b. The cause of loss for Sean is the lawsuit filed by John.
  c. Sean may need to pay general, special, and punitive damages as a result of the liability suit.

Educational Objective 4

4-1. The assets exposed to loss when an individual retires are the individual's regular employment income and the related benefits, such as health insurance.

4-2. The causes of loss associated with health and disability loss exposures are chronic illness and or physical or mental disability.

4-3. These are the four types of disability classifications:
- Temporary partial disability
- Temporary total disability
- Permanent partial disability
- Permanent total disability

4-4. a. Assets exposed to loss as the result of Anton's premature death include the expected income on which his wife and family rely.
  b. The financial cause of loss is the loss of the income that Anton could have earned he had remained alive. If replacement income from his life insurance, other financial assets, and Social Security do not meet his family's needs, it will likely experience considerable financial hardship.

Educational Objective 5

5-1. These are the six steps of the risk management process:
(1) Identify loss exposures
(2) Analyze loss exposures
(3) Examine the feasibility of risk management techniques
(4) Select the appropriate risk management techniques
(5) Implement the selected risk management techniques
(6) Monitor results and revise the risk management program

5-2. The loss characteristics that individuals and families may use to analyze their loss exposures are loss frequency, loss severity, total dollar losses, and timing of losses.

5-3. These are examples of measures individuals and families may use to implement selected risk management techniques:
- Purchasing loss reduction devices
- Contracting of loss prevention services
- Implementing loss control programs
- Obtaining expert advice on how to deal with challenging loss exposures
- Obtaining insurance policies on loss exposures not willing to be retained
- Creating a list of possessions subject to loss

5-4. The family might analyze its automobile loss exposures in this manner:
- First, it analyzes loss frequency. Four accidents over the last three years are a concern.
- Next, it analyzes loss severity. All four accidents were minor. Perhaps the family would consider maintaining higher collision deductibles on the two older-model cars. The family might retain the cost of minor accidents to avoid increased insurance premiums.
- It would then analyze total dollar losses. The four accidents were minor. However, the family should maintain high liability limits in case any of its members are subsequently involved in a serious auto accident. Even if one of the older cars has to be replaced instead of repaired, the cost of a new vehicle could be covered by family savings.
- Finally, it would analyze the timing of the accidents. Damage from the four accidents was easily repaired. However, the family still should account for the possibility of a future severe liability claim that may cost millions of dollars.

Educational Objective 6

6-1. The risk control techniques individuals and families use include these:
- Avoidance
- Loss prevention
- Loss reduction
- Separation
- Duplication
- Diversification

6-2. The risk financing techniques individuals and families use include these:
- Retention
- Transfer

6-3. A hold-harmless agreement is a noninsurance risk transfer in which one party assumes the legal liability of another party to the contract, such as in an apartment lease.

Hedging is another noninsurance risk transfer technique whereby on asset (money) is paid to offset the risk associated with another asset.

6-4. Loss prevention is a risk control technique that reduces the frequency of a particular loss, while loss reduction is a risk control technique that reduces the severity of a particular loss.

6-5. Planned retention is a deliberate assumption of loss that has been identified and analyzed. Unplanned retention is the inadvertent, unplanned assumption of a loss exposure that has not been identified or accurately analyzed.

6-6. a. Losses of low severity and low frequency are predictable and are usually of little financial consequence. These types of losses should be retained.

b. Costs of losses of high severity and low frequency are unpredictable and they present a high risk. These types of losses would likely be transferred before they occur.

c. Losses of low severity and high frequency are predictable. These types of losses should be retained by the family.

d. Loss exposures of medium severity and medium frequency may be retained or transferred, depending on tolerance for risk and the cost of the risk transfer.

Educational Objective 7

7-1. The risk financing techniques individuals and families use to manage their loss exposures are personal insurance, noninsurance transfers, and retention.

7-2. Personal insurance consists of three layers: social programs of insurance, group insurance, and individual insurance.

7-3. Property loss exposures stem from a legal interest in both real and personal property. Liability loss exposures originate from the possibility of being sued or being held responsible for someone else's injury.

7-4. Examples of the assets exposed to loss when an individual retires include regular employment income and the related benefits of employment, such as health insurance.

7-5. Methods individuals and families use to mitigate the financial consequences of retirement loss exposures include maintaining savings plans and pension plans to help them prepare for retirement. Social Security, an example of social insurance, is available for covered workers who are at least sixty-two years old. Other methods individuals and families may use to mitigate the financial consequences of retirement loss exposures include maintaining individual retirement accounts, employer- sponsored group pension plans, 401(k) savings plans and defined benefit plans.

7-6. An example of a premature death loss exposure is the expected income on which the deceased's family or heirs rely.

7-7. The needs-based approach attempts to estimate a family's future financial needs after considering any Social Security and other applicable benefits that the family would receive after the death of an income provider. The human life value approach attempts to measure the present value of the financial contribution of the wage earner to the family.

7-8. Health and disability insurance may be more important to an individual or family than life insurance because if a person becomes critically ill or disabled, the cost of hospital care, medication, and care giving could become a severe financial burden. The illness or disability may also prevent a spouse from obtaining employment that would help replace the income generated by the ill or disabled spouse.

7-9. A state may extend the period over which unemployed individuals can receive benefits if economic conditions or state unemployment rates warrant the extension.

7-10. The family might consider selecting from among social insurance, group insurance, and private insurance.

Social insurance provides a basic foundation of coverage. If Jerry, currently the only monetary provider for the family, were to die or become disabled, social insurance in the form of Social Security or workers compensation would likely be available to the family.

Group insurance (life insurance and health insurance) is provided by many employers. The family may augment its group coverage with individual insurance.

Individual insurance is insurance available for individuals and families for their homes and automobiles and other property and liability coverages. A liability umbrella can be purchased relatively inexpensively to cover extensive liability exposures, known as well as unknown.

Educational Objective 8

8-1. The policy declarations typically contain this information:
- Policy or policy number
- Policy inception and expiration dates (policy period)
- Name of the insurer
- Name of the insurance agent
- Name of the insured(s)
- Names of additional interests that are covered
- Mailing address of the insured
- Physical address and description of the covered property
- Numbers and edition dates of attached forms and endorsements
- Dollar amounts of applicable policy limits
- Dollar amounts of applicable deductibles
- Premium

8-2. Undefined words and phrases are interpreted according to these rules of policy interpretation:
- Everyday words are given their ordinary meanings.
- Technical words are given their technical meanings.
- Words with an established legal meaning are given their legal meanings.
- Consideration is given to local, cultural, and trade-usage meanings of words.

8-3. The insuring agreement is the promise of coverage the insurer makes to the insured and is essentially what the insured is buying.

8-4. A chart created to note the effect on coverage of each of the policy provision categories may read:

Policy Provision Category	Effect on Coverage
Declarations	Outline who or what is covered and where and when coverage applies
Definitions	May limit or expand coverage based on definitions of terms
Insuring agreements	Outline circumstances under which the insurer agrees to pay
Conditions	Outline steps insured needs to take to enforce policy
Exclusions	Limit insurer's payments based on excluded persons, places, things, or actions
Miscellaneous	Deal with the relationship between the insured and the insurer or establish procedures for implementing the policy

Educational Objective 9

9-1. For insureds, the primary source of information for generating scenarios for pre-loss policy analysis is their past loss experience. If the insured has not experienced a loss that triggered insurance coverage, friends, neighbors, co-workers, and family members can provide information about their experiences with losses and the claim process. The insurance producer and customer service representative are also good sources of information.

9-2. One of the limitations of scenario analysis is that, because the number of possible loss scenarios is theoretically infinite, it is impossible to account for every possibility.

9-3. The primary method of post-loss policy analysis is the DICE (an acronym representing the policy provision categories: declarations, insuring agreements, conditions, and exclusions) method, which is a systematic review of all the categories of property-casualty policy provisions.

9-4. The claims adjuster would follow the steps specified in the DICE decision tree to determine if the family's homeowners policy covered the loss.

First, he would check the declarations to see if anything found there would preclude coverage. If not, he would go to the next step.

Second, he would see if anything in the insuring agreement would preclude coverage. If not, he would go to the next step.

Third, he would check the conditions to see if anything precluded coverage. If not, he would go to the next step.

Fourth, he would check the exclusions and all other policy provisions not already analyzed, including the endorsements and miscellaneous provisions, to make sure that nothing would preclude coverage. If not, he would determine the amount payable under the policy.

Direct Your Learning

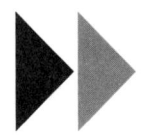

ASSIGNMENT 2

Automobile Insurance and Society

Educational Objectives

After learning the content of this assignment, you should be able to:

1. Identify each of the following approaches to compensating automobile accident victims and the advantages and disadvantages of each:
   - Tort liability system
   - Financial responsibility laws
   - Compulsory insurance laws
   - Uninsured motorists coverage
   - Underinsured motorists coverage
   - No-fault insurance

2. Describe no-fault automobile laws in terms of each of the following:
   - Types of no-fault laws
   - Benefits required by no-fault laws

3. Explain how high-risk drivers may obtain auto insurance.

4. Describe automobile insurance rate regulation in terms of each of the following:
   - Rating factors
   - Matching price to exposure
   - Competition

Study Materials

Required Reading:
- Personal Insurance
  - Chapter 2

Study Aids:
- SMART Online Practice Exams
- SMART Study Aids
  - Review Notes and Flash Cards—Assignment 2

2.1

Outline

- **Compensation of Auto Accident Victims**
  - A. Tort Liability System
    1. Advantages and Disadvantages of the Tort Liability System
  - B. Financial Responsibility Laws
    1. Advantages and Disadvantages of Financial Responsibility Laws
  - C. Compulsory Auto Insurance Laws
    1. Advantages and Disadvantages of Compulsory Auto Insurance Laws
  - D. Uninsured Motorists Coverage
    1. Advantages and Disadvantages of Uninsured Motorists Coverage
  - E. Underinsured Motorists Coverage
    1. Advantages and Disadvantages of Underinsured Motorists Coverage
  - F. No-Fault Automobile Insurance
    1. Advantages and Disadvantages of No-Fault Insurance

- **No-Fault Automobile Insurance**
  - A. Types of No-Fault Laws
    1. Modified No-Fault Plans
    2. Add-On Plans
    3. Choice No-Fault Plans
  - B. Benefits Required by No-Fault Laws

- **Automobile Insurance for High-Risk Drivers**
  - A. Voluntary Market Programs
  - B. Residual Market Programs
    1. Automobile Insurance Plans
    2. Joint Underwriting Associations (JUAs)
    3. Other Programs

- **Automobile Insurance Rate Regulation**
  - A. Rating Factors
    1. Primary Rating Factors
    2. Other Rating Factors
    3. Other Discounts and Credits
  - B. Matching Price to Exposure
  - C. Competition

- **Summary**

Study tips: Narrow the focus of what you need to learn. Remember, the Educational Objectives are the foundation of each of the Institutes' courses, and the exam is based on these Educational Objectives.

For each assignment, you should define or describe each of the Key Words and Phrases and answer each of the Review and Application Questions.

Educational Objective 1

Identify each of the following approaches to compensating automobile accident victims and the advantages and disadvantages of each:

- Tort liability system
- Financial responsibility laws
- Compulsory insurance laws
- Uninsured motorists coverage
- Underinsured motorists coverage
- No-fault insurance

Key Words and Phrases

Financial responsibility law

Compulsory auto insurance law

First party

Unsatisfied judgment fund

Uninsured motorists (UM) coverage

Underinsured motorists (UIM) coverage

No-fault automobile insurance

Review Questions

1-1. Briefly describe how the tort liability system compensates injured auto accident victims.

1-2. a. Describe three circumstances under which a motorist is required to provide proof of financial responsibility to comply with financial responsibility laws.

   b. Describe the disadvantages of financial responsibility laws.

1-3. Describe an advantage of compulsory insurance laws, as compared to financial responsibility laws.

1-4. Explain how low-cost auto insurance addresses the problem of uninsured drivers.

1-5. Describe the common characteristics of unsatisfied judgment funds.

1-6. Briefly describe how no-fault automobile insurance operates.

1-7. Explain why no-fault auto insurance laws were developed.

Application Question

1-8. Contrast uninsured motorists coverage (UM) with underinsured motorists coverage (UIM).

Educational Objective 2
Describe no-fault automobile laws in terms of each of the following:
- **Types of no-fault laws**
- **Benefits required by no-fault laws**

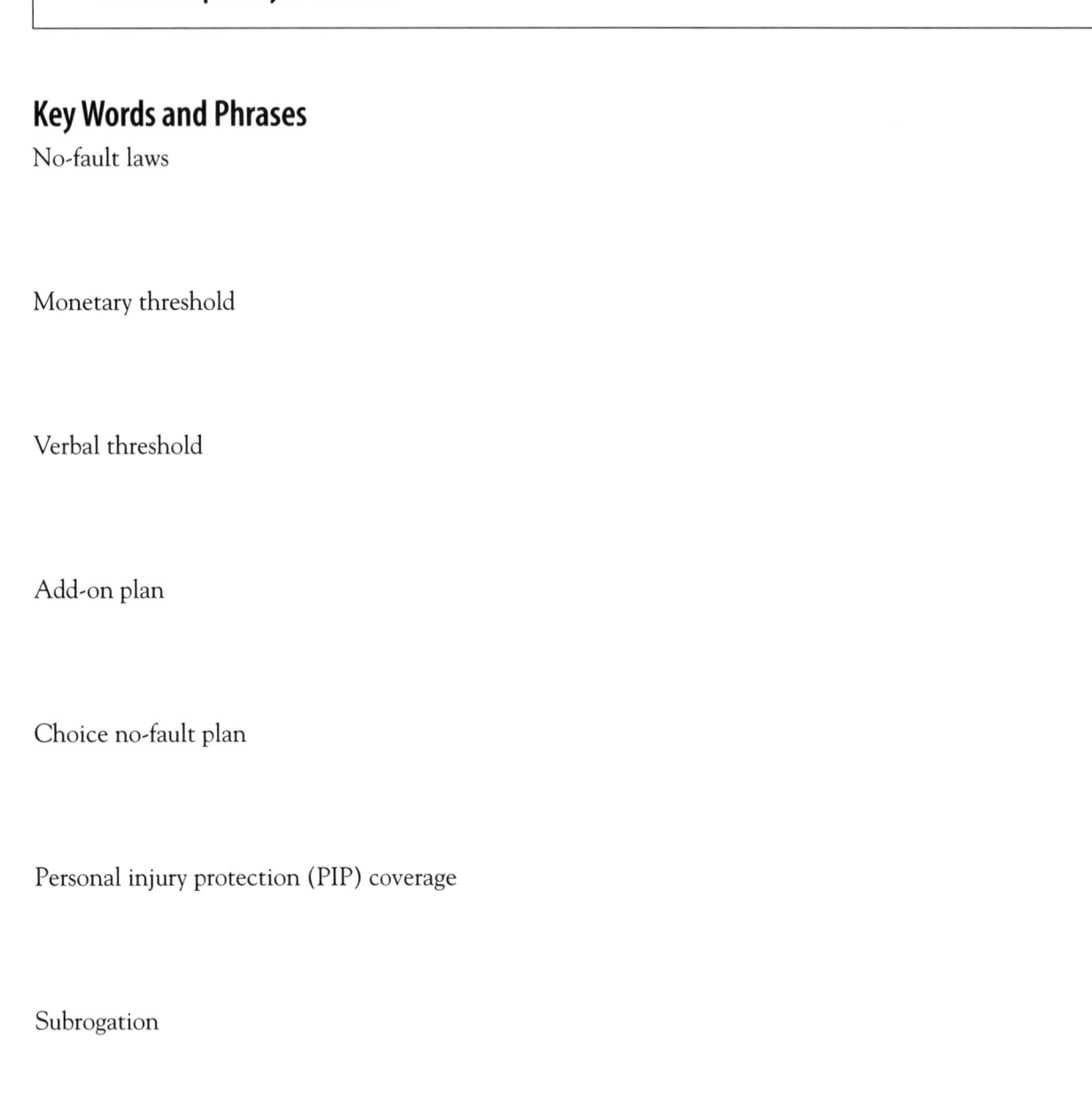

Key Words and Phrases

No-fault laws

Monetary threshold

Verbal threshold

Add-on plan

Choice no-fault plan

Personal injury protection (PIP) coverage

Subrogation

Review Questions

2-1. Contrast a pure no-fault system with modified no-fault plans.

2-2. How do add-on plans differ from choice no-fault plans?

2-3. Identify four benefits required by no-fault laws.

2-4. What determines the personal injury protection (PIP) coverage benefits that insurers provide?

Application Question

2-5. Tom lives in a modified no-fault state and carries the minimum PIP medical coverage limit of $20,000 set by the plan. Tom's state has a monetary threshold for noneconomic losses of $50,000. He sustains injuries in an auto accident and incurs $30,000 in economic losses. Tom also suffers $15,000 in noneconomic losses.

    a. What amount of economic losses would Tom collect from his own insurer?

b. What amount of noneconomic losses would Tom collect from his own insurer?

c. Can Tom sue the at-fault party for economic losses in this case? Explain your answer.

d. Can Tom sue the at-fault party for noneconomic losses in this case? Explain your answer.

Educational Objective 3
Explain how high-risk drivers may obtain auto insurance.

Key Words and Phrases
Residual market

Safe driver insurance plans (SDIPs)

Automobile insurance plan

Joint underwriting association (JUA)

Reinsurance facility

Rate

Review Questions

3-1. Identify two types of programs that provide automobile insurance for high-risk drivers.

3-2. How do the activities of insurers of high-risk drivers in the voluntary market differ from the activities of insurers in the residual market?

3-3. Under a state automobile insurance plan, how are the high-risk drivers apportioned to the auto insurers in that state?

3-4. What roles does a state joint underwriting association (JUA) serve with regard to rates, policy forms, and claim settlement for high-risk drivers?

Application Question

3-5. XYZ Auto Insurance sells insurance in a state that has a reinsurance facility for high-risk drivers. Mary is a high-risk driver who has obtained insurance from XYZ. XYZ, in turn, assigned Mary to the reinsurance facility. Mary subsequently had an auto accident and is responsible for the damage to Bill's auto and for Bill's injuries.

   a. Does XYZ or the reinsurance facility accept Mary's application and service her policy?

   b. Does XYZ or the reinsurance facility handle Bill's liability claim?

   c. What organization(s) bears any underwriting losses that result from Bill's liability claim?

Educational Objective 4

Describe automobile insurance rate regulation in terms of each of the following:

- Rating factors
- Matching price to exposure
- Competition

Review Questions

4-1. Explain these rating factors and why insurers use them:

   a. Territory

   b. Age (if permitted by state law)

   c. Driver education

   d. Multi-car policy

   e. Credit-based insurance score (if permitted by state law)

4-2. Describe the homogeneous classes or rating categories that insurers often use to help match price to exposure.

4-3. Explain the relationship between competition and regulatory monitoring of insurance rates and how that monitoring is accomplished.

Application Question

4-4. XYZ Insurance has its home office in a state with a population that consists predominantly of people of a particular ethnic origin. XYZ wanted to encourage state residents to buy insurance policies, so it filed rates with the state insurance regulators that extended a flat 70 percent discount to all applicants of the predominant ethnic origin, after considering other rating factors. Explain why the state regulators might not approve these rates based on each of the following rating objectives.

   a. Rates must be adequate to pay all claims and expenses.

   b. Rates must not be unfairly discriminatory.

… Automobile Insurance and Society 2.13

Answers to Assignment 2 Questions

NOTE: These answers are provided to give students a basic understanding of acceptable types of responses. They often are not the only valid answers and are not intended to provide an exhaustive response to the questions.

Educational Objective 1

1-1. If a driver operates an auto in a negligent manner that results in bodily injury to another person or in damage to another's property, the operator can be held legally liable for damages incurred by the injured person. Under the tort liability system, injured auto accident victims must prove that another party was at fault before they can collect damages from that party.

1-2. a. A motorist is required to provide proof of financial responsibility under these circumstances:
- After an auto accident involving bodily injury or property damage exceeding a certain dollar amount
- After a conviction for certain serious offenses, such as drunk driving or reckless driving, or after losing a driver's license because of repeated violations
- Upon failure to pay a final judgment that results from an auto accident

b. The disadvantages of financial responsibility laws include these:
- Most financial responsibility requirements become effective only after an accident, a conviction, or a judgment.
- Financial responsibility laws do not guarantee payment to all accident victims. Persons injured by uninsured drivers, hit-and-run drivers, or drivers of stolen cars might not be compensated.
- Injured persons might not be fully indemnified for their injuries even when injured by motorists who can prove financial responsibility. Most financial responsibility laws set minimum financial requirements, which may not fully compensate a victim.

1-3. An advantage of compulsory insurance laws, as compared to financial responsibility laws, is that motorists must provide proof of financial responsibility before an accident occurs. By requiring proof of financial responsibility prior to an accident, compulsory insurance laws go beyond financial responsibility laws by ensuring that accident victims are compensated for their losses.

1-4. Low-cost auto insurance is intended to decrease the number of uninsured drivers by making minimal liability coverage available at a reduced cost. Low-cost insurance programs are intended to provide some level of protection at a reduced cost to assist lower-income drivers in purchasing the insurance coverage required to comply with compulsory auto insurance laws.

1-5. Unsatisfied judgment funds have these characteristics:
- An injured person can receive compensation from the fund after having obtained a judgment against a negligent driver and proving that the judgment cannot be collected.
- The maximum amount paid is generally limited to the state's minimum compulsory insurance requirement. In addition, most funds reduce the amount paid by any amount the injured person has collected from other collateral sources of recovery, such as workers compensation benefits or insurance.

- The negligent driver is not relieved of legal liability when the unsatisfied judgment fund compensates the insured person. The negligent driver's license is revoked until the driver reimburses the fund.

1-6. Under a no-fault system, an injured person does not need to establish fault and prove negligence in order to collect payment for damages. In addition, certain no-fault laws place some restrictions on an injured person's right to sue a negligent driver who causes an accident. In some states, when a claim is below a certain monetary threshold, the injured motorist collects for injuries under his or her own insurance policy.

1-7. No-fault laws were developed to avoid the costly and time-consuming process of determining legal liability for auto accidents under the tort liability system. By eliminating the need to prove fault, no-fault laws allow accident victims to receive benefits much sooner after an accident and, as a result, may allow for a quicker recovery from injuries.

1-8. Uninsured motorists (UM) coverage compensates an insured for bodily injury caused by an uninsured motorist, a hit-and-run driver, or a driver whose insurer is insolvent. Underinsured motorists (UIM) coverage, on the other hand, provides additional limits of protection to the victim of an auto accident when the negligent driver's insurance limits are insufficient to pay for the damages.

Educational Objective 2

2-1. In a pure no-fault system, injured persons would not need to establish fault or prove negligence to collect payment for damages, but they also would not be able to seek damages through the tort liability system. In contrast, under a modified no-fault plan, injured persons would collect economic losses from their own insurers based on state-mandated PIP benefits, and they can sue at-fault drivers for any economic losses that exceed the no-fault coverage limits.

2-2. An add-on plan allows injured drivers the option of collecting for economic losses through their own insurer, but it places no restrictions on their right to sue a negligent party for damages. In contrast, a choice no-fault plan enables the insured to choose whether to be covered on a modified no-fault basis at the time the policy is purchased or renewed. Under a choice plan, insureds who choose the modified no-fault option have limitations on the right to sue for certain types of auto injuries. Insureds who do not choose the modified no-fault option retain full rights to seek compensation from the negligent party, but they pay a higher premium than those insureds who choose the modified no-fault option.

2-3. Benefits required by no-fault laws include these:
- Medical expenses
- Rehabilitation expenses
- Loss of earnings
- Expenses for essential services
- Funeral expenses
- Survivors' loss benefits

2-4. PIP benefits are determined by state no-fault laws.

2-5. a. Tom would collect $20,000 in economic losses from his own insurer because his PIP medical coverage is limited to $20,000 and his economic losses ($30,000) exceed the limit.

b. Under modified no-fault laws, insureds cannot collect for noneconomic losses through their PIP coverage, so Tom cannot collect from his insurer for his noneconomic losses.

c. Tom can sue the at-fault party for his economic losses that exceed the $20,000 paid by his insurer—the additional $10,000. To recover any additional losses, he must first prove that the other driver was at fault for the accident.

d. Because Tom's economic losses ($30,000) are below the $50,000 monetary threshold in this modified no-fault state, he cannot sue the at-fault party for his noneconomic losses.

Educational Objective 3

3-1. Two types of programs that provide automobile insurance for high-risk drivers are voluntary market programs and residual market programs.

3-2. Insurers of high-risk drivers in the voluntary market accept their own applications, service their policies, pay their claims and expenses, and retain full responsibility for their own underwriting results. Insurers of high-risk drivers in the residual market may accept applications and service policies, but responsibility for underwriting results is usually transferred to a pool or shared proportionally by all insurers in the market in one of several ways.

3-3. Under a state automobile insurance plan, all auto insurers doing business in the state are assigned their proportionate share of high-risk drivers based on the total volume of auto insurance written in the state.

3-4. The state JUA sets the insurance rates and approves the policy forms to be used for high-risk drivers. The JUA designates servicing insurers that settle claims of high-risk drivers.

3-5. a. XYZ accepts Mary's application and services her policy.

b. In servicing Mary's policy under the pool arrangement of the reinsurance facility, XYZ handles Bill's liability claim.

c. Because the state has a reinsurance facility, all private insurers doing business in the state share any underwriting losses that occur as a result of Bill's claim.

Educational Objective 4

4-1. a. Territorial factors include the location where the auto is used and garaged, road conditions, state safety laws, and the extent of traffic regulation. These factors affect the frequency and/or severity of loss.

b. Young drivers have less driving experience and tend to be involved in accidents more frequently than older drivers; therefore, rates for younger drivers are often higher than those for older drivers.

c. Young drivers who complete an approved driver education course (usually including road experience) often qualify for a premium discount. Drivers age fifty-five and older sometimes qualify for a premium discount for successfully completing defensive driver training courses. Driver training can help reduce the frequency and severity of auto losses.

- d. A discount is often given to policyholders with more than one auto insured under the same policy. Two or more autos owned by the same insured are usually not driven as often as a single auto, and it is less costly for the insurer to cover additional autos under the same contract, so savings may be passed to the insured.
- e. This numerical ranking is based on the individual's financial history (similar to a credit score, but without income data) and is sometimes used to determine insurance rates. Research shows that insureds with low insurance scores submit more claims than insureds with high scores.

4-2. Insurers often divide auto insurance applicants into homogeneous classes (rating categories) such as "preferred," "standard," and "nonstandard" that reflect different levels of exposure to loss. Applicants who have good driving records and rating factors present minimal loss exposure and, therefore, enjoy lower insurance rates. Conversely, applicants who have poor driving records or rating factors present greater loss exposure and are charged higher rates.

4-3. Intense competition among insurers prompts regulators to monitor rates carefully to ensure adequacy and reasonableness. Regulators monitor rates primarily through insurers' rate filings.

4-4.
- a. If a large number of applicants of the predominant ethnic origin had poor driving experience and/or numerous claims, a 70 percent discount on their rate would be unlikely to provide enough profit for the insurer to adequately pay its claims and expenses.
- b. A 70 percent discount on rates based on the applicant's ethnic origin is unfairly discriminatory to all other applicants because an individual's ethnicity does not affect his or her loss potential.

Direct Your Learning

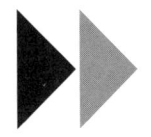

ASSIGNMENT 3

Personal Auto Policy: Liability, Medical Payments, and Uninsured Motorists Coverage

Educational Objectives

After learning the content of this assignment, you should be able to:

1. Summarize the sections of the Personal Auto Policy.

2. Identify the types of information typically contained on the declarations page of a personal auto policy.

3. Define the words and phrases included in the definitions section of the Personal Auto Policy.

4. Summarize each of the provisions in Part A—Liability Coverage of the Personal Auto Policy.

5. Given a case describing an auto liability claim, determine whether Part A—Liability Coverage of the Personal Auto Policy would cover the claim and, if so, the amount the insurer would pay for the claim.

6. Summarize each of the provisions in Part B—Medical Payments Coverage of the Personal Auto Policy.

7. Given a case describing an auto medical payments claim, determine whether Part B—Medical Payments Coverage of the Personal Auto Policy would cover the claim and, if so, the amount the insurer would pay for the claim.

8. Summarize each of the provisions in Part C—Uninsured Motorists Coverage of the Personal Auto Policy.

9. Describe underinsured motorists insurance in terms of:
   - Its purpose
   - The ways in which it can vary by state

10. Given a case describing an uninsured motorists claim, determine whether Part C—Uninsured Motorists Coverage of the Personal Auto Policy would cover the claim and, if so, the amount the insurer would pay for the claim.

Study Materials

Required Reading:
- Personal Insurance
  - Chapter 3

Study Aids:
- SMART Online Practice Exams
- SMART Study Aids
  - Review Notes and Flash Cards—Assignment 3

Outline

- **Overview of the Personal Auto Policy**
  - A. Declarations
  - B. Agreement and Definitions
  - C. Overview of Coverages
  - D. Endorsements
- **Declarations**
  - A. Insurer
  - B. Named Insured
  - C. Policy Period
  - D. Description of Insured Autos
  - E. Schedule of Coverages
  - F. Applicable Endorsements
  - G. Lienholder
  - H. Garage Location
  - I. Rating Information
  - J. Signature
- **Definitions**
- **Part A—Liability Coverage**
  - A. Insuring Agreement
    1. Damages and Defense Costs Covered
    2. Persons and Organizations Insured
  - B. Supplementary Payments
  - C. Exclusions
    1. Intentional Injury
    2. Property Owned or Transported
    3. Property Rented to, Used by, or in the Care of the Insured
    4. Bodily Injury to an Employee of an Insured
    5. Public or Livery Conveyance
    6. Garage Business Use
    7. Other Business Use
    8. Vehicle Used Without Reasonable Belief of Being Entitled
    9. Nuclear Energy Liability Losses
    10. Vehicles With Fewer Than Four Wheels or Designed for Off-Road Use
    11. Other Vehicles Owned by Insured or Available for Insured's Regular Use
    12. Vehicles Owned by or Available for Family Member's Regular Use
    13. Racing
  - D. Limit of Liability
  - E. Out of State Coverage
  - F. Financial Responsibility
  - G. Other Insurance
- **Part A—Liability Coverage Case**
  - A. Case Facts
  - B. Case Analysis Tools
  - C. Determination of Coverage
  - D. Determination of Amounts Payable
- **Part B—Medical Payments Coverage**
  - A. Insuring Agreement
  - B. Exclusions
    1. Motorized Vehicles With Fewer Than Four Wheels
    2. Public or Livery Conveyance
    3. Vehicles Used as a Residence or Premises
    4. Injury During the Course of Employment
    5. Other Vehicles Owned by Insured or Available for Insured's Regular Use
    6. Vehicles Owned by or Available for Family Member's Regular Use
    7. Vehicle Occupied Without Reasonable Belief of Being Entitled
    8. Vehicles Used in the Business of an Insured
    9. Bodily Injury From Nuclear Weapons or War
    10. Nuclear Radiation
    11. Racing
  - C. Limit of Liability
  - D. Other Insurance
- **Part B—Medical Payments Coverage Case**
  - A. Case Facts
  - B. Case Analysis Tools
  - C. Determination of Coverage
  - D. Determination of Amounts Payable
- **Part C—Uninsured Motorists Coverage**
  - A. Insuring Agreement
    1. Insured Persons
    2. Uninsured Motor Vehicles
  - B. Exclusions
    1. Owned But Not Insured Vehicle

2. Owned Vehicle With Primary UM Coverage in Other Policy
3. Claim Settlement That Prejudices Insurer's Right of Recovery
4. Public or Livery Conveyance
5. Vehicle Used Without Reasonable Belief of Being Entitled
6. No Benefit to Workers Compensation or Disability Benefits Insurer
7. Punitive Damages
C. Limit of Liability
D. Other Insurance
E. Arbitration

▶ **UM/UIM Endorsements and State Variations**
A. Purpose of Coverage
B. State Variations
1. Mandatory or Optional Coverage
2. Limits Trigger or Damages Trigger
3. Stacking

▶ **Part C—Uninsured Motorists Coverage Case**
A. Case Facts
B. Case Analysis Tools
C. Determination of Coverage
D. Determination of Amounts Payable

▶ **Summary**

Don't spend time on material you have already mastered. The SMART Review Notes are organized by the Educational Objectives found in each course guide assignment to help you track your study.

For each assignment, you should define or describe each of the Key Words and Phrases and answer each of the Review and Application Questions.

Educational Objective 1
Summarize the sections of the Personal Auto Policy.

Review Questions

1-1. List the information found on the declarations page of a Personal Auto Policy (PAP).

1-2. Identify the information contained in the Agreement and Definitions page of the PAP.

1-3. Contrast the coverage provided under Part A of the PAP with the coverage provided under Part D.

Application Question

1-4. At the renewal of his policy, George switched insurers for the PAP covering his family's vehicles. Explain how George can use the declarations page to compare the new policy with the policy from the previous insurer.

Educational Objective 2
Identify the types of information typically contained on the declarations page of a personal auto policy.

Key Words and Phrases

Named insured

Policy period

Vehicle identification number (VIN)

Review Questions

2-1. Describe the policy period for a PAP.

2-2. List the information that is included in the description of insured autos on the PAP.

2-3. Identify the rating information found on the PAP declarations page that may lead to reduced premiums.

Application Question

2-4. Amy is completing an application for a PAP and is not sure how to answer the question regarding the garage location for her vehicle. Explain what this term means and how it is used on the PAP.

Educational Objective 3
Define the words and phrases included in the definitions section of the Personal Auto Policy.

Key Words and Phrases

Collision coverage

Other than collision (OTC) coverage

Review Questions

3-1. Explain why some words or phrases included in the PAP are shown in quotation marks.

3-2. Explain how the definition of "you" and "your" provides coverage for a spouse of the named insured.

3-3. Describe the purpose of the "leased vehicles" definition in the PAP.

3-4. Describe the importance of the definition of "business" in the PAP.

Application Question

3-5. Janice lives in her own apartment and insures her car under a PAP. Her sisters, Dana and Louise, still live at home with their parents. Explain whether Dana and Louise are included as family members under Janice's auto coverage as defined in the PAP.

Educational Objective 4
Summarize each of the provisions in Part A—Liability Coverage of the Personal Auto Policy.

Key Words and Phrases
Prejudgment interest

Supplementary payments

Attachment

Postjudgment interest

Public or livery conveyance

Review Questions

4-1. Explain what occurs if the cost to defend an insured under the PAP exceeds the policy limit of liability.

4-2. In what situation would an insurer pay the cost of a bail bond for an insured under a PAP?

4-3. Explain the intent behind the PAP exclusion that eliminates liability coverage for an insured while employed or engaged in the business of selling, repairing, servicing, storing, or parking vehicles designed for use mainly on public highways:

Application Question

4-4. Sara works as a maid for Charlie. Charlie insures his auto under a PAP. He asks Sara to accompany him to the grocery store. While en route, he drives the car into a pole, causing bodily injury to Sara. Workers compensation benefits are not required for domestic employees in the state where the accident occurred. Explain what liability coverage Charles has for Sara's claims against him.

Educational Objective 5
Given a case describing an auto liability claim, determine whether Part A—Liability Coverage of the Personal Auto Policy would cover the claim and, if so, the amount the insurer would pay for the claim.

Application Questions

The student should assume that all the case facts remain the same as those in the Part A—Liability Coverage case study unless otherwise stated in a question. The student should also refer to the policy language provided in the case study's exhibits to answer a question.

5-1. Would the exclusion relating to whether a driver has a reasonable belief that the insured is entitled to use a vehicle in Sam's and George's PAPs apply if Sam's blood alcohol level did not exceed the legal limit at the time he demanded that George return his car keys? Explain your answer.

5-2. Assume that Sam's blood alcohol level did not exceed the legal limit at the time he demanded his car keys from George. Assume further that Sam and George were brothers living in the same household and therefore qualified as "family members" under each other's policy. Would an exclusion of Sam's PAP apply under these circumstances? Explain your answer.

5-3. Assume the car George was driving at the time of the accident was not Sam's car, but was instead a rental car that George was using as a temporary substitute while his car was being repaired. Assume further that the owner of the rental car carried an auto policy with a $15,000 limit of liability per person. How would that affect the Other Insurance provision of George's PAP?

5-4. The steering linkage of Sam's car broke, causing George to lose control of Sam's car and hit a bridge abutment. Later it was determined that the broken steering linkage resulted from defective parts. In a trial to determine liability, the jury still assessed George with 80 percent of the fault for the accident and awarded Sam $200,000 in damages for his injuries. The insurers paid their total limit of liability of $120,000 to Sam. George wants to appeal. Must Sam's and George's insurers continue to defend George? Explain your answer.

Educational Objective 6
Summarize each of the provisions in Part B—Medical Payments Coverage of the Personal Auto Policy.

Review Questions

6-1. Describe the two classes of insureds covered by Part B of the PAP.

6-2. Describe the exception to the PAP Part B exclusion that eliminates coverage for injuries sustained by an insured while occupying a vehicle (other than a covered auto) that is owned by or available for the regular use of a family member.

6-3. Explain how a coverage issue is resolved in a claim from a driver who has Part B coverage under a PAP and who was injured while driving a borrowed vehicle whose owner also has Part B coverage under a PAP.

Application Question

6-4. Elizabeth's son, Sam, is a family member as defined in his mother's PAP. Although Sam is old enough to drive, after having been involved in several serious accidents, he has promised his mother that he will not drive. However, late one Saturday night, Sam becomes bored and decides to go for a drive. He takes his mother's car while she is sleeping. While driving, he strikes a parked car and is injured. Explain what medical expense coverage Sam may have under Elizabeth's PAP.

Educational Objective 7

Given a case describing an auto medical payments claim, determine whether Part B—Medical Payments Coverage of the Personal Auto Policy would cover the claim and, if so, the amount the insurer would pay for the claim.

Application Question

The student should assume that all the case facts remain the same as those in the Part B—Medical Payments Coverage case study unless stated otherwise in a question. The student should also refer to the policy language provided in the case study's exhibits to answer a question.

7-1. Assume that, rather than striking another vehicle with his pickup truck, Jerry was struck by a car while walking to a customer's front door to deliver a pizza. How would Jerry's Medical Payments Coverage be affected?

7-2. How would Sara's Medical Payments Coverage be affected if she worked part-time for Jerry's restaurant as a cashier?

7-3. How would Sara's and Jerry's Medical Payments Coverage be affected if Sara's parents owned the pickup truck Jerry was driving at the time of the accident?

Educational Objective 8
Summarize each of the provisions in Part C—Uninsured Motorists Coverage of the Personal Auto Policy.

Key Word or Phrase
Arbitration

Review Questions
8-1. Describe the four categories of criteria a vehicle must meet to be covered by Part C of the PAP.

8-2. Explain the purpose of the PAP Part C exclusion that eliminates uninsured motorists (UM) coverage for a claim that the insured settles without the insurer's consent if such a settlement prejudices the insurer's right to recover payment.

8-3. Describe the Part C policy provision that is intended to prevent "stacking" of UM payments under a policy that covers more than one car owned by the named insured.

8-4. Explain whether a decision resulting from arbitration, the dispute resolution method designated by Part C of the PAP, is binding upon both parties when the amount of damages agreed on exceeds the minimum limit for bodily injury specified by the state's financial responsibility law.

Application Question

8-5. Doug is employed as a delivery driver for a pizza restaurant. When delivering pizza, he uses his own vehicle, which is insured under his PAP. Doug is seriously injured during a pizza delivery when his car is struck from behind by a hit-and-run driver. The pizza restaurant's workers compensation insurer, XYZ Insurance, pays Doug for his medical expenses and lost wages. XYZ Insurance decides to seek reimbursement from Doug's PAP insurer under Part C of Doug's policy. Explain the basis of XYZ's claim and what will likely occur in XYZ's attempt to assert it.

Educational Objective 9
Describe underinsured motorists insurance in terms of:
- **Its purpose**
- **The ways in which it can vary by state**

Review Questions

9-1. Describe the conditions in which underinsured motorists (UIM) coverage applies.

9-2. Aside from using ISO's Underinsured Motorists Coverage Endorsement (PP 03 11), explain how states can provide UIM coverage as a supplement to the UM coverage in the PAP.

9-3. Describe the key criterion that determines when a UIM endorsement with a limits trigger applies.

Application Question

9-4. Carol and Richard each live in a state that applies a damages trigger to a UIM endorsement. Carol has an auto liability policy with a $75,000 UIM limit. Richard purchased auto liability coverage with a $125,000 single limit. Richard causes an auto accident in which Carol is injured.

   a. Explain how Carol's UIM coverage will be affected if her damages amount to $200,000.

   b. Explain how Carol's UIM coverage will be affected if her damages amount to $100,000.

Educational Objective 10

Given a case describing an uninsured motorists claim, determine whether Part C—Uninsured Motorists Coverage of the Personal Auto Policy would cover the claim and, if so, the amount the insurer would pay for the claim.

Application Question

The student should assume all the case facts remain the same as those in the Part C—Uninsured Motorists Coverage case study unless stated otherwise in a question. The student should also refer to the policy language provided in the case study's exhibits to answer a question.

10-1. If Amanda was injured in a robbery attempt while her vehicle was disabled instead of being struck by an uninsured motor vehicle, how would that affect coverage for her injury claim in this case? Explain your answer.

10-2. Assume that, after Amanda signed a release of her claim against Rocky, her insurer discovered that Rocky has $250,000 in assets that it could have sought in order to recover payments it made to Amanda. How would that affect coverage?

10-3. Amanda and her insurer cannot agree on an amount to compensate her for her injuries. They agree to submit the dispute to arbitration. The arbiters award Amanda only enough to pay her medical bills and offer nothing for Harry's claim for loss of companionship claim. Explain Amanda's and Harry's options.

10-4. Assume Amanda's and Harry's PAP provides $50,000, instead of $250,000 in UM bodily injury coverage per accident. Amanda and Harry believe they should have two limits of coverage since they both have a claim (Amanda for her bodily injury and Harry for his loss of her companionship). They also believe that, because they have listed two vehicles in their policy's declarations and paid a separate premium for UM coverage for each vehicle, they should be entitled to two coverage limits. Are they right? Explain your answer.

Answers to Assignment 3 Questions

NOTE: These answers are provided to give students a basic understanding of acceptable types of responses. They often are not the only valid answers and are not intended to provide an exhaustive response to the questions.

Educational Objective 1

1-1. The declarations page of the PAP can include the name and mailing address of both the insurer and the named insurer, the policy period, and the name and address of the producer, if applicable. It also may include a description of the covered autos, limits of liability, premium and rating information, and any endorsements added to the policy.

1-2. The Agreement and Definitions page of the PAP includes a general agreement stating that the insurer is providing the coverage subject to payment of premium and to the terms of the policy. Definitions are also provided for words and phrases used throughout the policy.

1-3. Part A provides liability coverage and protects the insurer against claims for bodily injury or property damage arising out of the operation of an auto. Part D of the PAP covers physical damage to a covered auto and includes collision and other than collision coverages.

1-4. When comparing the two policies, George can look at the declarations page of each policy to review the dates of coverage, the descriptions of covered autos, limits of liability, endorsement listings, and premiums in order to determine whether any changes have been made and whether the information is accurate.

Educational Objective 2

2-1. The policy period starts at 12:01 AM standard time at the address of the policyholder on the date the policy becomes effective and ends at 12:01 AM standard time on the date the policy expires.

2-2. The description of insured autos usually includes the year, make, model, and vehicle identification number (VIN) of each covered vehicle. The description may also include the body type, annual mileage, use of the vehicle, and date of purchase.

2-3. Rating information that could qualify for premium discounts and lead to reduced premiums include the insured's having multiple cars insured under the policy, passing a driver training or defensive driving course, achieving a good scholastic record, or having a vehicle with passive restraints or anti-theft devices.

2-4. The garage location is the place where the auto is principally parked overnight. This location is used for rating purposes when calculating the premium for the policy.

Educational Objective 3

3-1. When a word or phrase is shown in quotation marks, this means that the definition for that word or phrase is included in the definitions section of the policy and that those definitions apply to the entire policy.

3-2. The words "you" and "your" also include an unnamed spouse of the named insured—provided that the spouse is a resident of the same household. When an unnamed spouse of the named insured moves out of the household but remains married to the insured, the spouse is considered "you" for another ninety days or until the policy expires—whichever comes first. Coverage ceases if the spouse is named on another policy.

3-3. The definition of "leased vehicles" clarifies what the policy includes when it refers to an owned auto. A leased private passenger auto, pickup, or van is deemed to be an owned auto if it is leased under a written agreement for a continuous period of at least six months.

3-4. The definition of this term is important in understanding exclusions that apply to the coverage parts in the PAP.

3-5. Neither Dana nor Louise would be included in the definition of family members under Janice's auto coverage because they do not reside in the same household as Janice. The PAP defines a family member as a person who is related to the named insured or spouse by blood, marriage, or adoption and who resides in the named insured's household.

Educational Objective 4

4-1. The insurer agrees to defend the insured and pay all legal costs the insured may incur in a liability suit—even if the combined costs exceed the limit of liability. In other words, the insurer is obligated to pay defense costs in addition to the policy limits.

4-2. The cost of a bail bond is covered under the PAP's Supplementary Payments provision. The insurer agrees to pay up to $250 for the cost of a bail bond (bail bond premium) required because of an accident that results in bodily injury or property damage covered by the policy.

4-3. The intent is to exclude a loss exposure that should be covered by a commercial auto policy, such as a garage policy purchased by the owner of the business.

4-4. The PAP excludes liability coverage for bodily injury to an employee of an insured who is injured during the course of employment. Sara is employed by Charlie, the insured, and was injured during the course of her employment. However, an exception to this exclusion is injury to a domestic employee in the course of employment when workers compensation benefits are not required. Therefore, despite the exclusion, Charlie's PAP should provide coverage for Sara's liability claim against him.

Educational Objective 5

5-1. This exclusion would probably apply. It states the insurer will not provide liability coverage for any insured using a vehicle without a reasonable belief that he or she is entitled to do so. If Sam's blood alcohol level did not exceed the legal limit, his judgment was probably not significantly impaired, and his attempt to revoke his earlier permission to George to drive his car should be effective. By refusing Sam's demand to return the car keys and by proceeding to drive Sam's car over Sam's objections, George appears to have known that he did not have Sam's permission to drive the car. Any belief that he had such permission might be deemed unreasonable. As a result, liability coverage for George under both his and Sam's policies would be probably excluded.

5-2. Exclusion A.8 of Part A of the PAP states that the exclusion does not apply to a "family member" (George) using a covered auto (Sam's car) that is owned by the named insured (Sam).

5-3. Under the Other Insurance provision of Part A of George's PAP, coverage for a nonowned vehicle while used as a temporary substitute, such as the rental car, is to be excess over any other collectible insurance. Therefore, for Sam's bodily injury claim, the insurer for the rental car owner will pay up to $15,000 as primary coverage and George's insurer will pay up to $100,000 as excess coverage. A total of $115,000 is available to cover Sam's injuries.

5-4. In many states, the insurers would not be required to continue to defend George. The PAP's Part A Insuring Agreement provision states an insurer's duty to defend ends when its limit of liability for the coverage has been exhausted by payments of judgments or settlements.

Educational Objective 6

6-1. Part B covers two classes of insureds:
- The named insured and "family members" (as defined in the PAP) are covered for their medical expenses if they are injured while occupying a motor vehicle or as pedestrians when struck by a motor vehicle designed for use mainly on public roads.
- Any other person while occupying a covered auto.

6-2. The exclusion does not apply to the named insured and spouse occupying such a vehicle.

6-3. For the driver of a nonowned vehicle, the driver's own PAP is excess over any other collectible auto insurance that pays medical or funeral expenses, including the PAP of the owner of the vehicle.

6-4. Part B of the PAP contains an exclusion that eliminates coverage if an insured sustains an injury while using a vehicle without a reasonable belief that he is entitled to do so. Taking his mother's car while she was sleeping and having made a previous promise that he would not drive would appear to place Sam within the application of this exclusion and preclude coverage for his injuries in this accident. However, the medical payments exclusion does not apply to a family member who uses an owned auto of the named insured. For insurance purposes, it is assumed that a family member has permission to use another family member's car. Therefore, Sam's medical expenses should be covered by his mother's PAP within the limits of her policy.

Educational Objective 7

7-1. Jerry's injuries would still be covered by his PAP even though he was not occupying a vehicle. The policy's Insuring Agreement provision states that a named insured is covered as a pedestrian when struck by a motor vehicle designed for use on public roads. However, the exclusion still applies that eliminates coverage for an accident that occurs during the course of employment if workers compensation benefits are required or available for the bodily injury. Therefore, Jerry would not have coverage because of this exclusion, but not because he was a pedestrian when he was injured.

7-2. The exclusion that eliminates coverage for an accident that occurs during the course of employment if workers compensation benefits are required or available for the bodily injury in Jerry's PAP may also apply if Sara was injured in the course of her employment. However, based on the facts given, it does not appear that the exclusion would apply. She was not acting as the restaurant's cashier when she was occupying Jerry's pickup at the time of the accident. Therefore, Jerry's policy should cover her medical expenses. Her coverage under her parents' policy would be unaffected by these facts for the same reason.

7-3. If Sara's parents owned the pickup, it would not be a covered auto under Jerry's policy, and she would not qualify as an insured under his policy. Therefore, the coverage from his policy would not be available to her. However, Sara's parents' policy would cover her medical expenses. Jerry would still not be covered under the exclusion that eliminates coverage for an accident that occurs during the course of employment if workers compensation benefits are required or available for the bodily injury. This same exclusion would eliminate coverage for Jerry under Sara's parents' policy.

Educational Objective 8

8-1. To be covered by Part C, a vehicle must be a land vehicle or trailer that meets any of these criteria:
- No bodily injury liability insurance or bond applies to the vehicle at the time of the accident.
- A bodily injury liability policy or bond is in force, but the limit for bodily injury is less than the minimum amount required by the state's financial responsibility law.
- The vehicle is a hit-and-run vehicle whose owner or operator cannot be identified.
- A bodily injury policy or bond applies at the time of the accident, but the insurance or bonding company (a) denies coverage or (b) is or becomes insolvent.

8-2. The purpose of this exclusion is to protect the insurer's right to assert a subrogation action against the party who is legally responsible for the insured's injuries.

8-3. The terms in the limit of liability provision are intended to prevent stacking. The terms state that the limits shown in the declarations are the most that will be paid regardless of the number of insured persons, claims made, vehicles or premiums shown in the declarations, or vehicles involved in the accident.

8-4. If the amount agreed on in arbitration exceeds the statutory limit, either party can demand the right to a trial within sixty days of the arbitrators' decision. Otherwise, the arbitrators' decision is binding.

8-5. In some states, if an injured employee receives workers compensation benefits, the workers compensation insurer has a legal right to recover the amount of the benefits from a negligent third party through subrogation. If an employee receives workers compensation benefits for an injury involving an uninsured, at-fault driver, the workers compensation insurer could sue the driver or attempt to make a claim under the injured employee's UM coverage, which is what XYZ Insurance is attempting to do. However, Part C of the PAP contains an exclusion that prevents any insurer from benefiting directly or indirectly under a workers compensation law. That exclusion will likely prevent XYZ from obtaining reimbursement under Doug's PAP UM coverage.

Educational Objective 9

9-1. Underinsured motorists (UIM) coverage applies when a negligent driver is insured for at least the minimum required financial responsibility limits but that driver's policy's liability limits are insufficient to pay the insured's damages.

9-2. Aside from using ISO's Underinsured Motorists Coverage Endorsement (PP 03 11), states can provide coverage as a supplement to the UM coverage in the PAP by using either a state-specific UIM endorsement or a single, state-specific endorsement providing both UM and UIM coverages that replaces the UM coverage of the standard PAP.

9-3. The key criterion for UIM protection with a limits trigger is that the liability limits of the other party's policy are less than the insured's UIM limits.

9-4. a. If Carol's damages amount to $200,000, her UIM coverage will be triggered because Richard's policy limit is less than Carol's damages.

   b. If Carol's damages amount to $100,000, her UIM coverage will not be triggered because her damages are less than Richard's limit.

Educational Objective 10

10-1. The Insuring Agreement provision of Part C—Uninsured Motorists Coverage of the PAP states that, for uninsured motorists coverage to apply, bodily injury must result from an accident that arises out of the ownership, maintenance, or use of an uninsured motor vehicle. Amanda's injuries were not caused by such a vehicle; therefore, her PAP would not cover her injuries. Harry's loss of companionship while Amanda was recovering is also not covered.

10-2. The PAP Part C Exclusion B eliminates uninsured motorists coverage for bodily injury sustained by an insured when the insured settles a bodily injury claim and such settlement prejudices the insurer's right to recover payment. In the original fact situation, the insurer concluded that it was not prejudiced by Amanda's $5,000 settlement with Rocky because Rocky had insufficient assets to reimburse it for the payments it made to Amanda for her medical expenses. However, if Rocky has $250,000 in obtainable assets, the settlement of $5,000 does prejudice the insurer's right of recovery. Amanda's insurer will probably exclude coverage for her injuries and Harry's claim as well.

10-3. Amanda and Harry could accept the arbiters' award of $100,000, which covers her medical bills. That amount is greater than the minimum limit for bodily injury specified by the financial responsibility law of her state. Consequently, per the terms of the Arbitration provision under her PAP's uninsured motorists coverage, the arbitration award is nonbinding. Therefore, Amanda and Harry have the option to pursue litigation against their own insurer for a higher award. However, litigation is a costly and sometimes lengthy process that can produce unexpected results.

10-4. Amanda and Harry are probably incorrect about their being entitled to two coverage limits under their PAP. The most their insurer would pay the couple for the sum of their damages would be the policy's applicable limit of liability. They cannot each separately collect up to the limit, because, according to the policy, the limit is the most the insurer will pay for bodily injury resulting from any one accident regardless of the number of insureds, claims made, vehicles or premiums shown in the declarations, or vehicle involved in the accident.

Direct Your Learning

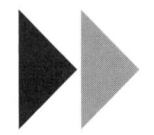

ASSIGNMENT 4

Personal Auto Policy: Physical Damage, Duties After an Accident, Endorsements, and General Provisions

Educational Objectives

After learning the content of this assignment, you should be able to:

1. Summarize each of the provisions in Part D—Coverage for Damage to Your Auto of the Personal Auto Policy.

2. Given a case describing an auto physical damage claim, determine whether Part D—Coverage for Damage to Your Auto of the Personal Auto Policy would cover the claim and, if so, the amount the insurer would pay for the claim.

3. Identify the insured's duties following an auto accident or loss (Part E) covered by the Personal Auto Policy.

4. Summarize each of the general provisions in Part F of the Personal Auto Policy.

5. Identify the Personal Auto Policy endorsements that are used to handle common auto loss exposures.

6. Given a case describing an auto claim, determine whether the Personal Auto Policy would cover the claim and, if so, the amount the insurer would pay for the claim.

Study Materials

Required Reading:
- Personal Insurance
  - Chapter 4

Study Aids:
- SMART Online Practice Exams
- SMART Study Aids
  - Review Notes and Flash Cards—Assignment 4

Outline

- **Part D—Coverage for Damage to Your Auto**
  - A. Insuring Agreement
    1. Collision Coverage
    2. Other Than Collision Coverage
    3. Nonowned Autos
    4. Deductibles
  - B. Transportation Expenses
  - C. Exclusions
    1. Public or Livery Conveyance
    2. Wear and Tear, Freezing, Breakdown, and Road Damage to Tires
    3. Radioactive Contamination or War
    4. Electronic Equipment
    5. Media and Accessories
    6. Government Destruction or Confiscation
    7. Trailer, Camper Body, or Motor Home
    8. Nonowned Auto Used Without Reasonable Belief of Being Entitled
    9. Radar and Laser Detection Equipment
    10. Customizing Equipment
    11. Nonowned Auto Used in Garage Business
    12. Racing
    13. Rental Vehicles
  - D. Limit of Liability
  - E. Payment of Loss
  - F. No Benefit to Bailee
  - G. Other Sources of Recovery
  - H. Appraisal
- **Part D—Coverage for Damage to Your Auto Case**
  - A. Case Facts
  - B. Case Analysis Tools
  - C. Determination of Coverage
  - D. Determination of Amounts Payable
- **Part E—Duties After an Accident or Loss**
  - A. General Duties
  - B. Additional Duties for Uninsured Motorists Coverage
  - C. Additional Duties for Physical Damage Coverage
- **Part F—General Provisions**
  - A. Bankruptcy of Insured
  - B. Changes in the Policy
  - C. Fraud
  - D. Legal Action Against the Insurer
  - E. Insurer's Right to Recover Payment
  - F. Policy Period and Territory
  - G. Termination
    1. Cancellation
    2. Nonrenewal
    3. Automatic Termination
    4. Other Termination Provisions
  - H. Transfer of Insured's Interest in the Policy
  - I. Two or More Auto Policies
- **Endorsements to the Personal Auto Policy**
  - A. Miscellaneous Type Vehicle Endorsement
  - B. Snowmobile Endorsement
  - C. Trailer/Camper Body Coverage (Maximum Limit of Liability)
  - D. Extended Non-Owned Coverage—Vehicles Furnished or Available for Regular Use
  - E. Named Non-Owner Coverage
  - F. Auto Loan/Lease Coverage
  - G. Limited Mexico Coverage
  - H. Excess Electronic Equipment Coverage
  - I. Coverage for Damage to Your Auto (Maximum Limit of Liability)
- **Personal Auto Coverage Case**
  - A. Case Facts
  - B. Case Analysis Tools
  - C. Determination of Coverage
  - D. Determination of Amounts Payable
- **Summary**

For each assignment, you should define or describe each of the Key Words and Phrases and answer each of the Review and Application Questions.

> ## Educational Objective 1
> Summarize each of the provisions in Part D—Coverage for Damage to Your Auto of the Personal Auto Policy.

Key Words and Phrases

Transportation expenses

Actual cash value (ACV)

Appraisal

Review Questions

1-1. John has collision coverage for his car. Another driver causes an accident that damages John's car. What are John's options for collecting damages?

1-2. How often can an insured drive a rented or borrowed auto and expect his or her auto physical damage insurance to cover the vehicle?

1-3. List three reasons for deductibles in auto physical damage coverage.

1-4. If an insured decides to race his sports car against the driver of another car on a city street, would damage to his car resulting from a collision that occurs during this activity be excluded under his PAP collision coverage?

Application Question

1-5. Jack rents a car from XYZ Rental Car Agency. He declines the damage waiver offered by XYZ at a substantial extra cost. While driving the rental car, Jack is involved in an auto accident with another car. Who is at fault is being contested, but, in the meantime, the rental car is not available to be rented while it is being repaired. XYZ has demanded reimbursement from Jack for its loss of the income the car would have earned in rental fees of $40 per day. Will Jack's PAP collision coverage for his covered auto help him in this situation and, if so, to what extent?

Educational Objective 2

Given a case describing an auto physical damage claim, determine whether Part D—Coverage for Damage to Your Auto of the Personal Auto Policy would cover the claim and, if so, the amount the insurer would pay for the claim.

Application Question

2-1. Lucia has a PAP with coverage for other than collision (OTC) loss that is subject to a $200 deductible. However, she did not purchase collision coverage and is not insured for those losses. What dollar amount, if any, will Lucia's insurer pay under her PAP for each of these losses? If a loss is not covered or not fully covered, explain why. Treat each loss separately.

   a. Lucia parks her car at the grocery store and goes shopping. She returns just in time to see another vehicle strike her car and then quickly leave. Assume that the state where Lucia's car is principally garaged in does not allow uninsured motorists property damage coverage. Her mechanic estimates that the repairs will cost $1,000.00.

   b. Lucia's factory-installed car radio valued at $400 was stolen from her car.

2-2. Tony has a PAP with coverage for OTC loss that is subject to a $500 deductible. After enjoying a night out at the movies with his friends, Tony discovers that his car has been stolen from the theatre parking lot. He immediately reports the loss to the police and to his insurer. The next morning, Tony rents a substitute auto for $40 a day. Thirty-six hours after the theft, the police report that they have found the car intact. Tony determines that the only items stolen were his compact disks (CDs), valued at approximately $500.

    a. What dollar amount, if any, will Tony's PAP pay for his rented auto?

    b. What dollar amount, if any, will Tony's PAP pay for the rented auto if his car was recovered after being missing for a total of seven days?

Educational Objective 3
Identify the insured's duties following an auto accident or loss (Part E) covered by the Personal Auto Policy.

Key Word or Phrase
Proof of loss

Review Questions

3-1. List the seven general duties a person seeking coverage under the PAP must perform after an accident or loss.

3-2. Describe the details a person seeking coverage under the PAP should include when notifying the insurer that an accident or loss has occurred.

3-3. Describe two additional duties required if the insured is seeking payment under Coverage C—Uninsured Motorists Coverage of the PAP.

4.8 Personal Insurance—INS 22

Application Question

3-4. Part E of a PAP states the general duties that the insured must perform after an accident or loss. Additional duties are required if the insured is seeking payment under Part D—Coverage for Damage to Your Auto.

   a. Explain why it is important for insureds to perform the duties after a loss as outlined in Part E of the PAP.

   b. Describe the three additional duties required if the insured is seeking payment under Part D of the PAP.

Educational Objective 4
Summarize each of the general provisions in Part F of the Personal Auto Policy.

Key Words and Phrases

Liberalization clause

Policy termination

Cancellation

Review Questions

4-1. Briefly describe each of the general provisions in Part F of the PAP:

   a. Bankruptcy of the Insured

   b. Policy Period and Territory

   c. Two or More Policies Issued by the Same Insurer

4-2. Identify four changes an insured can make during the policy period that can result in a premium increase or decrease.

4-3. Describe the obligations that an insured must fulfill before he or she can sue the insurer.

4-4. List the three reasons for which an insurer can cancel a policy that has been in force for sixty or more days.

Application Question

4-5. Explain how the PAP would respond in the following situations based on the provisions contained in Part F of the policy.

   a. The insured deliberately burns his car and submits a claim under the policy's physical damage coverage.

   b. Henry has replaced his current auto insurance policy with a new insurer. What must he do to cancel his original auto policy, which was issued by a different insurer?

Educational Objective 5
Identify the Personal Auto Policy endorsements that are used to handle common auto loss exposures.

Review Questions

5-1. Briefly describe the auto loss exposures covered by these endorsements to the PAP:

   a. Miscellaneous Type Vehicle Endorsement

   b. Trailer/Camper Body Coverage Endorsement

   c. Limited Mexico Coverage Endorsement

5-2. Identify four exclusions or modifications for liability coverage under the Snowmobile Endorsement.

5-3. Explain why an insured would need Excess Electronic Equipment Coverage.

5-4. List the items that are not included in loss payments under the Auto Loan/Lease endorsement.

Application Question

5-5. For each of these situations, recommend an appropriate endorsement that can be added to the PAP to meet the specified need.

   a. Daniel has two teenaged sons who own motorcycles. Daniel also has a large motor home that he uses for family vacations. He needs both liability and physical damage coverages on these vehicles.

b. Lucy does not own a car and relies primarily on public transportation. She does occasionally drive a friend's car and wants to rent a car while she is on vacation this summer. Lucy is concerned that she could be sued for a large amount if she were involved in an auto accident while driving such nonowned cars.

c. Phil works for the state and regularly drives a state-issued car to perform his duties. The state carries liability insurance on its vehicles, but Phil believes the liability limits carried by the state are inadequate.

d. Oscar owns a restored 1950s era vehicle that he displays at local vintage auto shows.

4.14 Personal Insurance—INS 22

> ## Educational Objective 6
> Given a case describing an auto claim, determine whether the Personal Auto Policy would cover the claim and, if so, the amount the insurer would pay for the claim.

Application Questions

The student should assume that all the case facts remain the same as those in the Personal Auto Coverage case study unless a question states otherwise. The student also should refer to the policy language provided in the case study's exhibits to answer a question.

6-1. If David had been operating a company-owned vehicle rather than his personal vehicle when the accident occurred, would his PAP cover the costs of the injuries to Wanda and her family?

6-2. The accident damaged several cartons of brochures and other property belonging to his employer that David was carrying. Does Part A of David's PAP include coverage for such property?

6-3. David had to rent a car while the damage to the vehicle was being repaired. Is the cost of such a rental covered under David's PAP?

Answers to Assignment 4 Questions

NOTE: These answers are provided to give students a basic understanding of acceptable types of responses. They often are not the only valid answers and are not intended to provide an exhaustive response to the questions.

Educational Objective 1

1-1. John can collect either from the other driver (or the driver's insurer) or from his own insurer. If John collects from his insurer, that insurer has the right to recover payment from the driver (or the driver's insurer). This recovery is referred to as subrogation.

1-2. The vehicle would be covered if driven occasionally by the insured. However, if the insured regularly drives the rented or borrowed vehicle, or if it is made available for the insured's regular use, the insured's coverage will not apply.

1-3. Insurers require deductibles in auto physical damage coverage for several reasons:
- To reduce small claims
- To hold down premiums
- To encourage insureds to be careful in protecting their cars against damage or theft

1-4. The damage to the insured's car would probably not be excluded. Loss to a covered auto is excluded if the auto is damaged while located in a facility designed for racing if the auto is being used to prepare for, practice for, or compete in any prearranged racing or speed contest. It appears that this race was not prearranged.

1-5. Part D of Jack's PAP provides coverage for transportation expenses. Under this provision, the rental car is covered as a nonowned auto, and the rental company's lost income while the car is being repaired is covered. However, the transportation expenses are limited to a maximum of $20 per day and $600 for each covered loss. Also, although transportation expenses do not have a dollar-amount deductible, they are subject to a waiting period a twenty-four-hour waiting period. Therefore, Jack's insurer would pay only $20 a day for XYZ's lost income, and the first day's loss would not be paid. Jack should also be aware that, at $20 per day and a maximum of $600, he only has thirty days of coverage ($600 divided by $20).

Educational Objective 2

2-1. a. In order for Lucia's PAP to cover these repairs, she would need collision coverage. Because Lucia has only other than collision coverage, her insurer will not cover the expense to repair her auto.

b. Because Lucia's radio was factory-installed, it is covered (less the deductible.) So her insurer will pay $200 ($400 minus $200) for the loss.

2-2. a. Tony's PAP imposes a two-day waiting period before transportation expense reimbursement begins. Because his car was recovered thirty-six hours after the theft, Tony's insurer will not cover the expense for the rental car.

b. Although the cost of renting a temporary substitute auto is insured under the Transportation Expenses coverage of Tony's PAP, that coverage is limited to $20 a day, not to exceed a maximum of $600. (The deductible does not apply to the Transportation Expense coverage.) The car was missing for a total of seven days. However, since the claim involves a total theft of the car, there is a two-day waiting period. Therefore, Tony will receive reimbursement of $100—$20 per day for his transportation expenses for five days to offset the $280 he paid for the rental car.

Educational Objective 3

3-1. A person seeking coverage under the PAP must perform seven duties:
- Provide prompt notification of the details of the accident or loss to the insurer.
- Cooperate with the insurer in the investigation, settlement, or defense of any claim or suit.
- Submit copies of notices or legal papers in connection with the accident or loss to the insurer.
- Agree to submit to a physical examination if requested by the insurer.
- Agree to be examined under oath if required by the insurer.
- Authorize the insurer to obtain medical reports and other pertinent records.
- Submit a proof of loss when required by the insurer.

3-2. The notification should include details such as how, when, and where the accident happened as well as the names and addresses of any injured persons and witnesses.

3-3. A person seeking benefits under Uninsured Motorists Coverage must perform two additional duties:
- Promptly notify the police if a hit-and-run driver is involved.
- Send a copy of the legal papers to the insurance company if the person seeking coverage sues the uninsured motorist.

3-4. a. It is important for insureds to perform the duties after a loss as outlined in Part E because if the insured does not perform them and this failure is prejudicial to the insurer, the insurer has no obligation to provide coverage and to pay for the loss.

b. There are three additional duties required if the insured is seeking payment under Part D of the PAP:
- The person seeking coverage must take reasonable steps after a loss to protect a covered auto or nonowned auto and its equipment from further loss.
- If a covered auto or nonowned auto is stolen, the person seeking coverage must promptly notify the police of the theft.
- The person seeking coverage must permit the insurer to inspect and appraise the damaged property before its repair or disposal.

Educational Objective 4

4-1. a. Bankruptcy of the Insured

This provision states that if the insured declares bankruptcy or becomes insolvent, the insurer is not relieved of any obligations under the policy.

b. Policy Period and Territory

According to this provision, coverage applies only to accidents and losses that occur during the policy period shown on the declarations page. The policy territory includes the United States, U.S. territories and possessions, Puerto Rico, and Canada. The policy also applies to a covered auto while being transported among ports of the U.S., Puerto Rico, or Canada. Coverage does not apply anywhere outside the policy territory.

c. Two or More Policies

According to this provision, if two or more auto policies issued to the named insured by the same insurer apply to the same accident, the insurer's maximum limit of liability is the highest applicable limit of liability under any one policy.

4-2. Changes an insured can make during the policy period that can result in a premium increase or decrease include changes:
- The number, type, or use of insured vehicles
- The operators using insured vehicles
- The place of principal garaging of insured vehicles
- The coverage provided, deductibles, or limits of liability

4-3. No legal action can be brought against the insurer until the insured has fully complied with all of the policy terms. In addition, under Part A—Liability Coverage, no legal action can be brought against the insurer unless the insurer agrees in writing that the insured has an obligation to pay damages or the amount of the insurer's obligation has been finally determined by a judgment after a trial.

4-4. The three reasons for which an insurer can cancel a policy that has been in force for sixty or more days are:
- The premium has not been paid.
- The driver's license of an insured has been suspended or revoked during the policy period (or since the last annual anniversary of the original effective date if the policy is for other than one year).
- The policy has been obtained by a material misrepresentation.

4-5. a. Because the PAP contains a fraud provision stating that no coverage exists for any insured that makes fraudulent statements or engages in fraudulent conduct in connection with any accident or loss for which a claim is made, the insurer would not be obligated to pay this claim.

b. To comply with the cancellation provision, Henry can cancel the original policy anytime during the policy period by returning the policy to the insurer or by giving advance written notice of the date the cancellation is to become effective.

Educational Objective 5

5-1. a. The Miscellaneous Type Vehicle endorsement provides coverage for a motor home, a motorcycle or similar type of vehicle, an all-terrain vehicle, a dune buggy, or a golf cart, all of which are not included within the definition of covered auto under the PAP.

b. The Trailer/Camper Body Coverage (Maximum Limit of Liability) endorsement covers direct and accidental loss to a trailer or camper body described in the Declarations of the policy or the schedule of the endorsement.

c. This endorsement extends the PAP coverages to an insured who is involved in an accident or loss in Mexico within twenty-five miles of the United States border on a trip of ten days or less. The coverage provided by this endorsement, however, does not meet Mexico's auto liability insurance requirements and the endorsement is effective only if primary liability coverage is also purchased from a licensed Mexican insurer.

5-2. The liability coverage for snowmobiles has four exclusions or modifications:
- Coverage does not apply if the snowmobile is used in any business.
- Coverage does not apply when the snowmobile is used in a race or speed contest or in practice or preparation for a race, regardless of whether the race is prearranged or organized.
- Coverage is excluded for any person or organization, other than the named insured, while renting or leasing a snowmobile.
- A passenger hazard exclusion can be activated, which excludes liability for bodily injury to any person while occupying or being towed by the snowmobile.

5-3. This coverage is needed because the unendorsed PAP excludes loss to any electronic equipment that is not permanently installed in the vehicle and also excludes loss to tapes, records, disks, or other media. The PAP also includes a $1,000 limit on electronic equipment that reproduces, receives or transmits audio, visual or data signals that are permanently installed in locations not used for that purpose by the auto manufacturer. The Excess Electronic Equipment endorsement can be used to increase the limit on such equipment from $1,000 to a limit shown in the endorsement schedule for insureds who have such equipment in their vehicles.

5-4. Under the Auto Loan/Lease endorsement, none of these would be included in any loss payment:
- Lease or loan payments that were overdue at the time of loss
- Penalties imposed under a lease for excessive use, abnormal wear and tear, or high mileage
- Security deposits not refunded by a lessor
- Costs for extended warranties; credit life insurance; or health, accident, or disability insurance purchased with the loan or the lease
- Balances transferred from previous loans or leases

The endorsement schedule includes a description of the covered auto(s) and premiums for other than collision and/or collision coverage.

5-5. a. The Miscellaneous Type vehicle endorsement could be used to provide liability and physical damage coverage for the two motorcycles and for the motor home.

b. Lucy could purchase a PAP with a Named Non-Owner Coverage Endorsement, which would provide liability, medical payments, and uninsured and underinsured motorists coverages. This coverage would apply when she uses a friend's car or operates a rental car. The endorsement does not include physical damage coverage.

c. Phil could purchase Extended Non-Owned Coverage as an endorsement to his PAP. The liability coverage provided by the endorsement is excess over the coverage already provided for the state-issued car.

Personal Auto Policy: Physical Damage, Duties After an Accident, Endorsements, and General Provisions 4.19

d. The Coverage for Damage to Your Auto (Maximum Limit of Liability) endorsement to the PAP could be used to establish the car's insurable value when the policy is written by inserting a stated amount of insurance in the policy. Under this endorsement (often called a "stated amount" endorsement), each vehicle is described, and a stated amount of insurance is shown that applies to collision loss and other than collision loss.

Educational Objective 6

6-1. No, the costs of the injuries to Wanda and her family would be paid by David's employer and the costs of the damage to the vehicles would be covered under a commercial auto policy.

6-2. No, Part A excludes coverage for property damage to property owned or being transported by the insured.

6-3. Yes, Part D—Coverage for Damage to Your Auto includes Transportation Expenses coverage, which provides up to a maximum of $600 for temporary transportation expenses not exceeding $20 per day in the event of a collision loss.

s.m.a.r.t. tips — Reduce the number of Key Words and Phrases that you must review. SMART Flash Cards contain the Key Words and Phrases and their definitions, allowing you to set aside those cards that you have mastered.

SEGMENT B

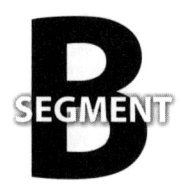

Assignment 5	Homeowners Property Coverage
Assignment 6	Homeowners Liability Coverage
Assignment 7	Homeowners Coverage Forms and Endorsements
Assignment 8	Other Residential Insurance
Assignment 9	Other Personal Property and Liability Insurance

Segment B is the second of three segments in the INS 22 course. These segments are designed to help structure your study.

Direct Your Learning

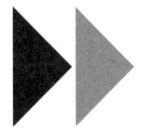

Assignment 5

Homeowners Property Coverage

Educational Objectives

After learning the content of this assignment, you should be able to:

1. Describe how individuals and families can use the ISO Homeowners insurance program to address their personal risk management needs.

2. Summarize the factors and adjustments important to rating homeowners insurance.

3. Describe the structure of the Homeowners policy (HO-3).

4. Summarize each of the HO-3 policy provisions in the following Section I—Property Coverages:

   - Coverage A—Dwelling
   - Coverage B—Other Structures
   - Coverage C—Personal Property
   - Coverage D—Loss of Use
   - Additional Coverages

5. Summarize each of the HO-3 policy provisions in Section I—Perils Insured Against.

6. Summarize each of the HO-3 policy provisions in Section I—Exclusions.

7. Summarize each of the HO-3 policy provisions in Section I—Conditions.

8. Given a case describing a homeowners property claim, determine whether the HO-3 Policy Section I—Property Coverages would cover the claim, and if so, the amount the insurer would pay for the claim.

Study Materials

Required Reading:
- Personal Insurance
  - Chapter 5

Study Aids:
- SMART Online Practice Exams
- SMART Study Aids
  - Review Notes and Flash Cards—Assignment 5

Outline

- **ISO Homeowners Program**
- **Homeowners Policy Rating Factors**
    - A. Base Premium Factors
    - B. Base Premium Adjustments
    - C. Final Adjustments
- **HO-3 Policy Structure**
    - A. Declarations
    - B. Agreement and Definitions
        1. Agreement
        2. Definitions
    - C. Section I—Property Coverages
    - D. Section II—Liability Coverages
    - E. Endorsements
- **HO-3 Section I—Property Coverages**
    - A. Coverage A—Dwelling
    - B. Coverage B—Other Structures
    - C. Coverage C—Personal Property
        1. Special Sublimits
        2. Property Not Covered
    - D. Coverage D—Loss of Use
    - E. Additional Coverages
- **HO-3 Section I—Perils Insured Against**
    - A. Insured Perils Under Coverages A and B: Direct Physical Loss
        1. Perils Excluded
        2. Exception to Perils Excluded—Water Damage Coverage
        3. Ensuing Losses Covered
    - B. Perils Insured Against for Coverage C
        1. Named Perils
        2. Named Perils Covered
- **HO-3 Section I—Exclusions**
    - A. Section I—Exclusions
        1. Ordinance or Law
        2. Earth Movement
        3. Water Damage
        4. Power Failure
        5. Neglect
        6. War
        7. Nuclear Hazard
        8. Intentional Loss
        9. Governmental Action
    - B. Perils Excluded for Coverages A and B Only
        1. Weather Conditions
        2. Acts or Decisions
        3. Faulty Workmanship
- **HO-3 Section I—Conditions**
    - A. Insurable Interest and Limit of Liability
    - B. Your Duties After Loss
    - C. Loss Settlement
        1. Coverage C—Personal Property and Miscellaneous Items
        2. Coverage A—Dwelling and Coverage B—Other Structures
    - D. Loss to a Pair or Set
    - E. Appraisal
    - F. Other Insurance and Service Agreement
        1. Other Insurance
        2. Service Agreement
    - G. Suit Against Us
    - H. Our Option
    - I. Loss Payment
    - J. Abandonment of Property
    - K. Mortgage Clause
    - L. No Benefit to Bailee
    - M. Nuclear Hazard Clause
    - N. Recovered Property
    - O. Volcanic Eruption Period
    - P. Policy Period
    - Q. Concealment or Fraud
    - R. Loss Payable Clause
- **HO-3 Section I—Property Coverage Case**
    - A. Case Facts
    - B. Case Analysis Tools
    - C. Determination of Coverage
    - D. Determination of Amounts Payable
- **Summary**

For each assignment, you should define or describe each of the Key Words and Phrases and answer each of the Review and Application Questions.

Educational Objective 1
Describe how individuals and families can use the ISO Homeowners insurance program to address their personal risk management needs.

Key Words and Phrases

Named perils coverage

Special form coverage

Functional replacement cost basis

Review Questions

1-1. Describe the typical insured whose risk management needs would be met by these homeowners insurance forms:

   a. HO-2

   b. HO-3

c. HO-4

d. HO-5

e. HO-6

f. HO-8

1-2. What is the difference between special form coverage and named peril coverage?

1-3. What is the primary difference in coverage between the HO-6—Unit-Owners Form and the HO-4—Contents Broad Form?

Application Question

1-4. David changed the oil in his car and left the pan of oil on the floor of the garage. While he was at work, his children walked across the floor where some oil had spilled and left oil-stained tracks on the living room wall-to-wall carpet and on the couch in the family room. Explain how HO-2, HO-3, HO-5, and HO-8 policies would respond to these losses.

Educational Objective 2
Summarize the factors and adjustments important to rating homeowners insurance.

Key Word or Phrase
Building Code Effectiveness Grading Schedule (BCEGS)

Review Questions

2-1. Describe how insurers typically develop a homeowners policy premium.

2-2. Describe the two broad classifications of construction used to determine the homeowners base premium.

2-3. What are package policy credits?

Application Question

2-4. Kate and her brother Dave recently purchased new homes. Kate's house, of masonry construction, is located in a large city that has its own fire department. Dave's house, of frame construction, is located in a rural area several miles from the city. Fire protection is provided by a volunteer fire company located five miles from Dave's home. With reference to each of the main rating factors, explain why Kate and Dave are likely to pay different premium amounts for their homeowners policies.

Educational Objective 3
Describe the structure of the Homeowners policy (HO-3).

Review Questions

3-1. What information is provided on the declarations page of the HO-3 policy?

3-2. What promises are made by the insurer and the insured in the policy's Insuring Agreement?

3-3. What information is included in Section I and Section II of the HO-3 policy?

3-4. What coverages may be included in the Additional Coverages section of an HO-3 policy?

Application Question

3-5. Bob owns and resides in a home that is insured with an unendorsed HO-3 policy. His mother, Carol, and his wife and daughter also live in the home. A fire erupted on the deck and destroyed Carol's cedar chest, which was property stored in the attached garage.

   a. Is Carol an insured under the policy? In what sections of the policy would this information be found?

   b. Is Carol's property covered under Bob's HO-3 policy? In what sections of the policy would this information be found?

> **Educational Objective 4**
> Summarize each of the HO-3 policy provisions in the following Section I—Property Coverages:
> - **Coverage A—Dwelling**
> - **Coverage B—Other Structures**
> - **Coverage C—Personal Property**
> - **Coverage D—Loss of Use**
> - **Additional Coverages**

Review Questions

4-1. Should an insured consider the land value at the residence premises when determining the amount of insurance to purchase?

4-2. What are three exclusions to coverage in the HO-3 under Coverage B—Other Structures?

4-3. Explain the purpose of personal property special sublimits in the HO-3.

Application Question

4-4. An HO-3 policy has a dwelling limit of $240,000. A fire (covered peril) in the insured's home destroys jewelry and a firearms collection.

　　a. What is the maximum coverage that can be provided for Coverages B, C, and D?

　　b. Would any special limits of liability apply to the jewelry and firearms?

Educational Objective 5
Summarize each of the HO-3 policy provisions in Section I—Perils Insured Against.

Key Word or Phrase

Ensuing loss

Review Questions

5-1. Describe the approach of HO-3 Section I—Property Coverages to perils insured against for direct physical loss under Coverages A and B and the intent of that approach.

5-2. Describe each of these HO-3 Section 1 exclusions that apply to Coverages A and B:

   a. Freezing of a plumbing, heating, air conditioning or sprinkler system, or a household appliance

   b. Theft of construction materials

   c. Mold, fungus, or wet rot

   d. Animals

5-3. Describe the water damage coverage exception to perils excluded under the HO-3 Section I.

5-4. Explain how the perils insured against under Coverage C of the HO-3 Section I differ from the perils insured against under Coverages A and B.

5-5. List those perils that personal property is insured against in Coverage C of the HO-3 Section I.

Application Question

5-6. Julie has an HO-3 policy to insure her home, detached garage, and personal property. Identify the appropriate coverages and explain whether the coverage(s) would insure her property against these perils (after any applicable deductible):

a. During a windstorm, a large tree branch fell through the roof and into Julie's living room, damaging the exterior and interior of her home, a sofa, and a coffee table. Rain that blew through the opening in the wall caused water damage to the carpeting.

b. Julie returned home one afternoon to find cracks and a hole in both panes of her bay window. Inside the home, an expensive vase was smashed and a large, steel spike lay in the middle of the room.

c. Julie's power company has been known to have power surges. One day a power surge damaged Julie's central air conditioner, the components of her personal computer, and her projection television system.

d. Julie left her new puppy in her detached garage during the day. When she returned home, the puppy had chewed the wooden door, the woodwork around the doorway, the cable for a television, a table leg, and three pairs of shoes.

Educational Objective 6
Summarize each of the HO-3 policy provisions in Section I—Exclusions.

Key Word or Phrase
Concurrent causation

Review Questions

6-1. Identify the three perils excluded from HO-3 Section I—Exclusions, Coverages A and B only.

6-2. Under what conditions does the HO-3 Section I Additional Coverages section add limited ordinance or law coverage back into the policy?

6-3. Explain why loss of spoiled food is excluded from coverage if it results from a power outage after a storm blows down power lines a few miles from an insured resident's premises.

Application Question

6-4. Rochelle's water heater exploded, resulting in extensive water damage to her home. She stayed with friends while repairs were being made. Upon returning home, she discovered that someone had broken into her home and had stolen several personal items. Explain whether the theft would be covered under Rochelle's HO-3 policy.

Educational Objective 7
Summarize each of the HO-3 policy provisions in Section I—Conditions.

Key Word or Phrase

Insurable interest

Review Questions

7-1. Under the Section I—Conditions of the HO-3 policy, what duties does an insured have after a property loss?

7-2. Identify the two ways losses to personal property listed under Coverage C—Personal Property in the HO-3 are settled.

7-3. Under the HO-3 Section I—Conditions, what options are available when an item that is part of a pair or set is damaged or destroyed?

7-4. Describe the appraisal process under Section I—Conditions of the HO-3 and the steps that are followed if appraisers' estimates differ.

7-5. Describe the rights that the Mortgage Clause in the HO-3 Section I—Conditions provides to a mortgagee.

7-6. Briefly summarize each of these Section I conditions of the HO-3:

   a. Insurable interest and limit of liability

   b. Abandonment of property

   c. Recovered property

   d. Concealment or fraud

   e. Loss payable clause

Application Questions

7-7. The Smiths own a home with a replacement cost of $400,000. The home is covered under an HO-3 with a Coverage A—Dwelling limit of $360,000. Lightning strikes the central air conditioner unit in the home and destroys it beyond repair. The unit has a useful life of ten years, a replacement cost of $10,000, and is now five years old.

   a. Determine the loss settlement for the air conditioning unit.

   b. Determine the loss settlement for the central air conditioning unit if the Smiths' HO-3 had a Coverage A limit of $180,000.

7-8. Kim and Dan Henessey own a home. Kim has an HO-3 with a $100,000 Coverage A limit. Dan also purchased a homeowners policy with a $150,000 Coverage A limit for the home.

   A natural gas explosion destroyed the couple's home, which had a replacement cost of $200,000 at the time of the loss. After the explosion, the Henesseys discover that two policies cover their home. A total of $250,000 in coverage is available. Calculate the amount that each policy will pay the Henesseys.

Educational Objective 8

Given a case describing a homeowners property claim, determine whether the HO-3 Policy Section I—Property Coverages would cover the claim, and if so, the amount the insurer would pay for the claim.

Application Questions

The student should assume that all the case facts remain the same as those in the HO-3 Policy Section I—Property Coverages case study unless a question states otherwise. The student also should refer to the policy language provided in the case study's exhibits to answer a question.

8-1. Assume that Lashonda's engagement ring (valued at $7,500) was in a part of the house unaffected by the fire. While she and Marvin were staying in a nearby hotel, a burglar broke into their home and stole the ring. Determine whether this loss would be covered under the HO-3 policy, and if so, for how much. Ignore any deductible that might apply.

8-2. In addition to the other damages from the fire, Marvin and Lashonda submitted a $1,200 claim to their insurer for one month's mortgage payment on their home that was due during the time they stayed at the hotel. Determine whether this loss would be covered under the HO-3 policy, and if so, for how much. Ignore any deductible that might apply.

Answers to Assignment 5 Questions

NOTE: These answers are provided to give students a basic understanding of acceptable types of responses. They often are not the only valid answers and are not intended to provide an exhaustive response to the questions.

Educational Objective 1

1-1. These are the typical insureds for each form:
   a. HO-2—Owner-occupants who are willing to accept named peril coverage in return for a lower premium
   b. HO-3—Owner-occupants of dwellings who would like broader coverage than that of the HO-2 on their dwellings and other structures
   c. HO-4—Tenants and other occupants of apartments or dwellings
   d. HO-5—Owner-occupants of dwellings who would like the broadest coverage available
   e. HO-6—Owners-occupants of condominium units and cooperative apartment shares
   f. HO-8—Owners-occupants who may not meet insurer underwriting standards required for other policy forms

1-2. Special form coverage protects property against direct physical loss that is not otherwise excluded by the coverage form.

   Named peril coverage protects property against direct physical loss for causes of loss listed and described in an insurance policy.

1-3. The primary difference in coverage between the HO-6 and the HO-4 is that the HO-6 form includes special provisions for loss exposures inherent in condominium and cooperative unit ownership.

   The various homeowners policies' responses to these losses would differ based on the coverages they provide:
   - The HO-2 form is a named perils policy. Because it does not include this type of loss as a named peril, the HO-2 does not cover the damage to the carpet and the couch.
   - The HO-3 form provides special form coverage for the dwelling. Because wall-to-wall carpet is part of the dwelling and is not excluded by the policy, the damage to the carpet would be covered at replacement cost. The damage to the couch would not be covered because dwelling contents are covered on a named perils basis.
   - The HO-5 provides special forms coverage for the dwelling and contents; therefore, the damage to the carpet and the couch would be covered.
   - The HO-8 form is a named peril policy. Because it does not include this type of loss as a named peril, the HO-8 does not cover the damage to the carpet and the couch.

1-4. The various homeowners policies' responses to these losses would differ based on the coverages they provide:
   - The HO-2 form is a named perils policy. Because it does not include this type of loss as a named peril, the HO-2 does not cover the damage to the carpet and the couch.

- The HO-3 form provides special form coverage for the dwelling. Because wall-to-wall carpet is part of the dwelling and is not excluded by the policy, the damage to the carpet would be covered at replacement cost. The damage to the couch would not be covered because dwelling contents are covered on a named perils basis.
- The HO-5 provides special forms coverage for the dwelling and contents; therefore, the damage to the carpet and the couch would be covered.

Educational Objective 2

2-1. An insurer applies base premium factors to develop the base premium, adjusts the premium based on individual risk management and loss exposure needs, and develops the final premium by using final adjustments, which can vary by insurer.

2-2. Two broad construction classifications are used to determine the homeowners base premium:
- Frame—includes structures with exterior walls of wood or other combustible construction
- Masonry—includes structures with exterior walls of combustible construction veneered with brick or stone, or masonry material

2-3. Package policy credits are policy discounts insurers sometimes offer to customers who place more than one line of business with them. These credits are one of several adjustments that insurers apply to develop the final homeowners premium.

2-4. Dave and Kate will likely pay different premiums because of the different rating factors applied by the insurer when developing the premium, including these:
- Dwelling location—Loss exposures in a city would be different from those in a rural area.
- Public protection class—Lynn's city fire department and Dave's volunteer fire company would be ranked according to the level of protection they provide
- Construction factors—Lynn's masonry construction would present different loss exposures than Dave's frame construction.

Educational Objective 3

3-1. The declarations page of the HO-3 policy provides information about the insured, the insured's residence, policy coverage limits, premium, Section 1 deductible, effective date, and forms and endorsements applied to the policy.

3-2. In the Insuring Agreement, the insurer agrees to provide coverage and the insured agrees to pay the premium and comply with the policy conditions.

3-3. Section I—Property Coverages specifies the property covered, the perils for which the property is covered, and the exclusions and conditions that affect property coverages and losses.

Section I includes these coverages:
- Coverage A—Dwelling: resident premises
- Coverage B—Other Structures: not attached to the dwelling, such as sheds, garages, and swimming pools
- Coverage C—Personal Property: anywhere in the world, including luggage and borrowed property.

- Coverage D—Loss of Use: exposure to financial loss apart from property damage
- Additional Coverages: such as debris removal and reasonable repairs

Section II—Liability Coverages includes personal liability coverage for third parties injured or whose property is damaged by an insured and medical payments to others within three years of an injury.

3-4. The Additional Coverages section applies to additional coverages provided, subject to certain limitations, such as debris removal, reasonable repairs, property removed, loss assessment, and ordinance or law.

3-5. a. The definition of insured is found in the Definitions section of the policy. Because Carol is a relative of the insured who resides full time in the named insured's household, she is considered an insured.

b. Section I, Coverage C would specify personal property covered in the policy. Carol's personal property would be covered by the HO-3 policy.

Educational Objective 4

4-1. An insured need not consider the land value at the residence premises because the land is specifically excluded from property coverage.

4-2. Coverage B—Other Structures excludes these structures:
- A structure rented to anyone who is not a resident of the dwelling (unless it is rented as a private garage)
- A structure from which any business is conducted
- A structure used to store business property solely owned by the insured or a tenant of the dwelling, other than gaseous or liquid fuel

4-3. Sublimits limit the amount of coverage available for losses to specified items, particularly high valued items or items that may be a target for theft. The smaller limits are intended to provide adequate dollar amounts of coverage for exposures of a typical family.

4-4. a. Maximum coverages for this covered loss include:
- Coverage B—Other Structures: $24,000 (up to 10 percent of Coverage A)
- Coverage C—Personal Property: $120,000 (up to 50 percent of Coverage A)
- Coverage D—Loss of Use: $72,000 (up to 30 percent of Coverage A)

b. No special limits would apply to the jewelry and firearms. The special limits for jewelry and firearms apply only if theft is the cause of loss. In this case, the cause of loss was fire.

Educational Objective 5

5-1 Under the HO-3 Section I, a broad statement of coverage against direct physical loss under Coverages A and B is followed by a statement that lists the excluded perils. Any peril that is not listed in these exclusions is covered. This approach provides coverage for a broad range of perils.

5-2 a. Freezing can cause pipes and hoses to burst or leak and cause extensive damage. If an insured fails to take reasonable precautions against freezing, coverage is excluded under Coverages A and B for any resulting damage.

b. Building materials and supplies for a home under construction are often targeted by thieves. Theft in or to a dwelling under construction or of construction materials and supplies is excluded under Coverages A and B until the dwelling is finished and occupied.

c. Coverage for loss resulting from these causes is excluded under Coverages A and B unless the mold, fungus, or rotting is hidden and results from an accidental leak of water or steam from a plumbing, heating, or air conditioning system or household appliance or from a storm drain or water, steam, or sewer pipes off the residence premises.

d. The HO-3 does not cover damage to animals under Coverages A and B because they are not covered property. The HO-3 also excludes damage caused by animals that an insured owns or keeps, or by birds, vermin, rodents, or insects.

5-3 Unless otherwise excluded, the HO-3 covers water damage to buildings or other structures that results from an accidental discharge or overflow of water or steam. The water or steam must come from a plumbing, heating, air conditioning, or sprinkler system; from a household appliance on the residence premises; or from a storm drain or water, steam, or sewer pipe off the residence premises. Coverage is provided for damage caused by the water and the cost of tearing out and replacing any part of the building or other structure necessary to make repairs. The loss to a damaged system or appliance is not covered.

5-4 The perils insured against under Coverage C differ significantly from the special form (open perils) coverage provided under Coverages A and B. Under Coverage C, only named perils (listed in the coverage form) are covered.

5-5. Personal property is insured against these perils in Coverage C:
- Fire or lightning
- Windstorm or hail
- Explosion
- Riot or civil commotion
- Aircraft
- Vehicles
- Smoke
- Vandalism or malicious mischief
- Theft
- Falling objects
- Weight of ice, snow, or sleet
- Accidental discharge or overflow of water or steam
- Sudden and accidental tearing apart, cracking, burning, or bulging
- Freezing
- Sudden and accidental damage from artificially generated electrical current
- Volcanic eruption

5-6. a. Windstorm is not an excluded peril under Coverage A, so coverage would be provided for the exterior and interior damage to Julie's home. Windstorm is a named peril under Coverage C, so coverage would be provided for the damage to Julie's sofa and coffee table. Because wind (a specified peril) caused the branch to damage the structure, leaving an opening that allowed the rain into the home, the water damage to the carpeting would be covered under Coverage C.

b. Because the source of the spike was unknown and no exclusion applies to this loss under Coverage A, replacement of the broken window panes would be covered. The vase would also be covered because Coverage C specifies falling objects and vandalism or malicious mischief as covered perils.

c. Because no applicable exclusion exists under Coverage A, the losses to Julie's central air conditioner would be covered. Although Coverage C lists the covered peril of sudden and accidental damage from artificially generated electric current, it makes an exception for losses to computers and home entertainment equipment. Therefore, the Coverage C losses resulting from the power surge would not be covered.

d. Because Coverage B specifically excludes damage caused by animals that an insured owns or keeps, no coverage is provided for the garage door or woodwork. Because Coverage C does not list an animal peril, no coverage is provided for damage to the cable, the table, or the shoes.

Educational Objective 6

6-1. The three perils excluded for Coverages A and B are weather conditions; acts or decisions any person, group, organization, or governmental body; and faulty workmanship.

6-2. The HO-3 Additional Coverages section adds limited ordinance or law coverage back into the policy, but only in relation to covered buildings or structures that have been damaged as a result of an insured peril. For these structures, the additional coverage applies to losses resulting from any ordinance or law that requires additional construction, demolition, remodeling, renovation, or repair, beyond the typical repairs to restore the structures after a loss.

6-3. Coverage for the spoiled food is excluded because the power failure occurred off the residence premises. If power had been interrupted by an insured peril that occurred on the insured's premises, the loss of the spoiled food would have been covered.

6-4. The Water Damage exclusion eliminates coverage for losses caused by flood, surface water, waves, and water or water-borne material such as sewage that backs up through sewers and drains. However, ensuing losses from fire, explosion, or theft resulting from water damage are covered. Therefore, Rochelle would have coverage for this loss.

Educational Objective 7

7-1. Following a loss that is or might be covered under the HO-3, the insured has these duties:
- Give prompt notice to the insurer
- Notify the police (for theft losses)
- Notify the credit card (or other appropriate) company, if a credit card is involved
- Protect the property from further damage
- Cooperate with the insurer
- Prepare an inventory
- Verify the loss
- Sign a sworn proof of loss

7-2. Losses to personal property under Coverage C—Personal Property are settled at the lesser of either the actual cash value (ACV) or the amount required to repair or replace the items.

7-3. When an item that is part of a pair or set is damaged or destroyed, the insurer may either replace the missing item for its actual cash value (ACV) or pay the insured the difference between the ACV of items as a pair and the ACV of the remaining single item.

7-4. During the appraisal process, the insurer and the insured each choose an appraiser to prepare an estimate of the value of the loss. Each party pays for its own appraiser. If the estimates differ, the two appraisers submit their differences to an umpire. The umpire is an impartial individual (often another appraiser or a judge) who resolves the differences. An agreement by any two of the three will set the amount of loss. The insurer and the insured share the cost of the umpire.

7-5. The Mortgage Clause condition establishes the rights of the mortgagee listed on the declarations page:
- If a loss occurs to property covered by Coverage A—Dwelling or Coverage B—Other Structures, the loss is payable jointly to the mortgagee and the insured.
- A mortgagee has rights that are independent of the insured's rights. If the insurer denies the insured's loss, the mortgagee retains the right to collect from the insurer its insurable interest in the property.
- An insurer must mail notice of cancellation or nonrenewal of a policy to the mortgagee (in addition to notice sent to the insured) at least ten days before the cancellation or nonrenewal.

7-6. a. The Insurable Interest and Limit of Liability condition limits the maximum payment for any single loss to the applicable limits shown on the Declarations page, regardless of the number of insureds who have an insurable interest in the property. This condition further limits loss payment to any insured to the extent of that insured's insurable interest in the property at the time of the loss.

b. The Abandonment of Property condition provides that if the insured abandons the property after it is damaged or destroyed, the insurer need not take over responsibility for it.

c. The Recovered Property condition provides that if the insurer pays a claim for the loss of property, and the property is later recovered, the insured has the option of taking the property and returning the claim payment or keeping the claim payment and allowing the insurer to take over the property.

d. The Concealment or Fraud condition states any insured who conceals or misrepresents any material information, engages in fraudulent conduct, or makes false statements relating to the insurance is not covered under the policy. This condition applies whether the conduct occurred before or after a loss.

e. In this policy provision, the insurer agrees to include the named loss payee when a claim is paid involving that personal property.

7-7. a. The Smith's home is insured for more than 80 percent of the replacement cost ($360,000 is 90 percent of $400,000). Therefore, the Smiths would receive $10,000 to replace the unit.

b. The Smiths' home is insured for less than 80 percent of the replacement cost. They would receive the greater of these values:
- The ACV of the air conditioner. The ACV would be the $10,000 replacement cost minus depreciation. If the central air conditioner has a useful life of ten years and is now five years old, this air conditioner would depreciate by 50 percent. The ACV would equal $5,000.

- The proportion of the cost to repair or replace the damage that the limit of insurance bears to 80 percent of the replacement cost: $180,000/ (0.80 × $400,000) × $10,000 = $5,625.

The Smiths, then, would receive the greater amount: $5,625.

7-8. The two losses will share the loss proportionally:
- The insurer that issued Kim's policy will pay 40 percent of the loss ($100,000 ÷ $250,000), or $80,000 (0.40 × $200,000).
- The insurer that issued Dan's policy will pay 60 percent of the loss ($150,000 ÷ $250,000), or $120,000 (0.60 × $200,000).

Educational Objective 8

8-1. Because the loss of Lashonda's ring is the result of theft, the special limit of liability of $1,500 would be paid.

8-2. Marvin and Lashonda would not be reimbursed for their mortgage payment because the Additional Living Expenses provision covers only the necessary and increased expenses caused by the temporary relocation.

Consult the registration booklet that accompanied this course guide for complete information regarding exam dates and fees. Plan to register with the Institutes well in advance of your exam. If you have any questions, or need updated registration information, contact the Institutes (see page iv).

Direct Your Learning

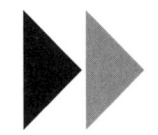

Assignment 6

Homeowners Liability Coverage

Educational Objectives

After learning the content of this assignment, you should be able to:

1. Summarize each of the HO-3 Policy provisions in the following Section II—Liability Coverages:
   - Coverage E—Personal Liability
   - Coverage F—Medical Payments to Others
   - Section II—Additional Coverages
2. Summarize each of the HO-3 policy provisions in Section II—Exclusions.
3. Summarize each of the HO-3 policy provisions in Section II—Conditions.
4. Summarize each of the HO-3 policy provisions in Sections I and II—Conditions.
5. Given a case describing a homeowners liability claim, determine whether the HO-3 Policy Section II—Liability Coverages would cover the claim, and, if so, the amount the insurer would pay for the claim.

Study Materials

Required Reading:
- Personal Insurance
  - Chapter 6

Study Aids:
- SMART Online Practice Exams
- SMART Study Aids
  - Review Notes and Flash Cards—Assignment 6

Outline

- **HO-3 Section II—Liability Coverages**
  - A. Coverage E—Personal Liability
  - B. Coverage F—Medical Payments to Others
  - C. Section II—Additional Coverages
    1. Claim Expenses
    2. First Aid Expenses
    3. Damage to Property of Others
    4. Loss Assessment
- **HO-3 Section II—Exclusions**
  - A. Section II—Exclusions Applying to Coverages E and F
    1. Motor Vehicle Liability
    2. Watercraft Liability
    3. Aircraft Liability
    4. Hovercraft Liability
  - B. Coverage E—Personal Liability and Coverage F—Medical Payments to Others
    1. Expected or Intended Injury
    2. Business
    3. Professional Services
    4. Insured's Premises Not an Insured Location
    5. War
    6. Communicable Disease
    7. Sexual Molestation, Corporal Punishment or Physical or Mental Abuse
    8. Controlled Substance
  - C. Exclusions That Apply Only to Coverage E—Personal Liability
    1. Loss Assessment and Contractual Liability
    2. Damage to the Insured's Property
    3. Damage to Property in the Insured's Care
    4. Bodily Injury to Persons Eligible for Workers Compensation Benefits
    5. Nuclear Liability
    6. Bodily Injury to an Insured
  - D. Exclusions That Apply Only to Coverage F—Medical Payments to Others
    1. Residence Employee Off Premises
    2. Bodily Injury Eligible for Workers Compensation Benefits
    3. Nuclear Reaction
    4. Injury to Residents
- **HO-3 Section II—Conditions**
  - A. Section II—Conditions Applying to Coverages E and F
    1. Limit of Liability
    2. Severability of Insurance
    3. Duties After "Occurrence"
    4. Duties of an Injured Person—Coverage F—Medical Payments to Others
    5. Payment of Claim—Coverage F—Medical Payments to Others
    6. Suit Against Us
    7. Bankruptcy of an Insured
    8. Other Insurance
    9. Policy Period
    10. Concealment or Fraud
- **HO-3 Sections I and II—Conditions**
  - A. Liberalization Clause
  - B. Waiver or Change of Provision Condition
  - C. Cancellation Condition
  - D. Nonrenewal Condition
  - E. Assignment Condition
  - F. Subrogation Condition
  - G. Death Condition
- **HO-3 Section II—Liability Coverage Case**
  - A. Case Facts
  - B. Case Analysis Tools
  - C. Determination of Coverage
  - D. Determination of Amounts Payable
- **Summary**

s.m.a.r.t. tips

Actively capture information by using the open space in the SMART Review Notes to write out key concepts. Putting information into your own words is an effective way to push that information into your memory.

For each assignment, you should define or describe each of the Key Words and Phrases and answer each of the Review and Application Questions.

> ## Educational Objective 1
> Summarize each of the HO-3 Policy provisions in the following Section II— Liability Coverages:
> - Coverage E—Personal Liability
> - Coverage F—Medical Payments to Others
> - Section II—Additional Coverages

Key Words and Phrases

Third party

Bodily injury

Property damage

Review Questions

1-1. Describe the general coverage provisions under the HO-3 Section II Coverage E—Personal Liability Coverage.

1-2. What determines the amount that the insurer will pay for damages under Coverage E?

1-3. For defense cost coverage under Coverage E, must the insured be found liable for damages? Explain your answer.

1-4. Explain when the insurer's obligation to defend an insured under Coverage E ends.

1-5. Describe the coverage that is provided and the expenses that are paid under Coverage F—Medical Payments to Others.

1-6. How does Coverage F differ from Coverage E?

1-7. List the claim expenses that the insurer may pay under the HO-3 Section II—Additional Coverage on the insured's behalf in addition to any judgment or settlement.

1-8. Describe the coverage for Damage to Property of Others provided under Section II—Additional Coverages.

Application Question

1-9. Richard has an HO-3 policy to insure his home, personal property, and liability. He shares his home with his ten-year-old son, Josh. For each of these situations, explain whether coverage would be provided under Section II—Liability Coverages and, if so, identify the applicable coverage(s):

   a. The family's one-year-old German shepherd, who often escapes from its enclosure, ran into their neighbor's yard and attacked their three year-old daughter. The girl suffered serious bite wounds on her face and arms.

   b. Josh invited his friend Tommy to their home to play catch one evening under Richard's supervision. Tommy tossed the ball straight up, intending to catch it. However, because the sun shone in his eyes, the ball instead hit Tommy in the face, breaking his glasses and cutting his cheek. Richard used a bandage and ice pack from his personal first-aid kit to treat Tommy's injuries and then called Tommy's parents. Tommy's cut required stitches and resulted in $700 in medical expenses. The cost to replace Tommy's glasses was $300.

c. Richard was required to join a homeowners association when he bought his home. The association owns a clubhouse. A guest at the clubhouse became permanently disabled after he fell down the stairs. The loss settlement for the claim exceeded the liability limit of the association's policy, so each member was assessed $5,000.

d. Richard borrowed his brother's golf cart for a weekend golf tournament. While his friend Sam was riding in the back of the cart, Richard stopped the cart abruptly on a hill and jumped out, failing to properly set the parking brake. The cart rolled down the hill and into a tree, severely damaging the cart. Sam jumped out of the cart before it hit the tree, but he dislocated his shoulder when he hit the ground, requiring medical attention and an emergency room bill of $300. Sam will only seek reimbursement of his medical bills.

Educational Objective 2
Summarize each of the HO-3 policy provisions in Section II—Exclusions.

Review Questions

2-1. What is the intent of the Motor Vehicle Liability exclusion in HO-3 Section II and what exception exists?

2-2. When an insured owns a small, low-powered watercraft that is never used in any organized racing events, what other criteria would exclude coverage under the Watercraft Liability exclusion to HO-3 Section II?

2-3. The HO-3 excludes all aircraft liability under Coverages E and F. However, model airplanes and hobby aircraft that do not carry people or cargo are covered. Explain why this exception applies to the Section II exclusion.

2-4. Describe the Expected or Intended Injury exclusion that applies to Coverages E and F.

2-5. What types of business activities are exceptions to the HO-3 Coverage E and F Business exclusion?

2-6. Explain the circumstance in which the HO-3 Coverage E and F Insured's Premises Not an Insured Location exclusion would apply to a guest who is injured at a vacation home owned by the insured.

2-7. Provide three examples of communicable diseases that are excluded from liability under Coverages E and F.

2-8. An insured mother frequently belittled her pre-teen daughter's best friend, Jan. Jan became despondent and attempted suicide. Assuming Jan's parents became aware of the insured's mental abuse, explain whether liability Coverages E and F under the insured's HO-3 would apply for Jan's injuries.

2-9. While under the influence of methamphetamine, the insured stabbed a store attendant. Explain whether liability Coverages E and F under the insured's HO-3 would apply for the injured victim.

2-10. What is the net impact under the HO-3 Loss Assessment exclusion under HO-3 Coverage E and the Section II—Additional Coverage with regard to liability losses assessed against policyholders who are members of a homeowners or condominium association or corporation?

2-11. Explain the reason for the Damage to the Insured's Property exclusion under Coverage E?

2-12. Explain how a state law requiring workers compensation benefits for domestic workers would affect coverage under the HO-3 Coverage E.

Application Question

2-13. Terry and Paula own a home with a four-stall detached garage and insure it under an HO-3 policy. Their eight-year-old daughter, Stacy, lives with them as does Holly, their twenty-eight-year-old resident nanny. Their state law requires that homeowners provide workers compensation benefits for domestic workers. For each of these situations, explain which of the HO-3 Section II Exclusions should be considered and whether they affect the HO-3 coverage:

   a. Terry rents a stall of his garage to a neighbor, Virginia, for her private auto for $35 per month during the winter.

   b. Stacy sold lemonade from a stand along their street one afternoon. Stacy inadvertently added a harmful fluid to the lemonade. A customer required a trip to the emergency room for treatment immediately after drinking the tainted lemonade.

c. Paula is an accountant and prepares income taxes for personal clients each year in her spare time. Paula miscalculated some figures on a tax return she prepared for a client. The error was not found until two years later. The client was required to pay penalties and interest to the federal and state governments totaling $7,000.

d. While the family stayed as guests in a friend's vacation cabin, Terry left a burner unattended when he answered a telephone call and started a small grease fire. The fire damaged the pan and the cupboard above the stove and the wall coverings, carpeting, curtains, and upholstery in the cabin were smoke-damaged. Stacy found the fire burning and tried to put it out; but she spilled hot grease on her leg, causing third-degree burns.

e. While she was off-duty, Holly went to a movie downtown with a friend. After crossing the street by the theatre, Holly tripped on a curb and broke her ankle.

Educational Objective 3
Summarize each of the HO-3 policy provisions in Section II—Conditions.

Key Word or Phrase

Loss assessment

Review Questions

3-1. As described in the HO-3 Section II Limit of Liability condition, explain how the limit of Coverage E—Personal Liability and of Coverage F—Medical Payments to Others on the declarations page applies when numerous people are injured in the same occurrence.

3-2. Explain the operation of the Severability of Insurance condition under Section II of the HO-3 in conjunction with the limit of liability.

3-3. Under the HO-3 Section II—Conditions, what are the insured's duties after an occurrence?

3-4. Describe the Duties of an Injured Person condition under Section II Coverage F.

3-5. Describe the Payment of Claim condition under Coverage F in conjunction with the intent of that coverage.

3-6. According to the Suit Against Us condition under the homeowners policy, what provision protects the insurer with respect to Coverage E?

3-7. Explain how the Other Insurance condition for Section II Coverage E applies when other insurance exists.

3-8. Explain how the Section II Concealment or Fraud condition would apply to an innocent insured who was not involved in the concealment or fraud.

Application Question

3-9. Anthony has an HO-3 policy to insure his home, personal property, and liability. He shares his home with his Aunt Mabel, who is an insured under the policy. For each of these situations, explain any applicable policy conditions and how the coverage would be affected:

   a. Mabel's dog escaped one afternoon and entered a nearby grocery store, where he was inadvertently shut in a cooler. The dog destroyed several cases of frozen meat and other goods and damaged the shelving before the grocery staff found him. Mabel retrieved her dog and the grocery store filed a suit against Mabel and Anthony, individually, for $8,000 each in damages for the loss of product and the loss of use of the cooler. When the legal documents arrived, Mabel notified the insurer of the claim circumstances and forwarded her documents to the insurer; but Anthony failed to forward his legal documents. The grocery store won the suit against Mabel and Anthony. The court found Mabel liable for $12,000 in damages and Anthony liable for $8,000.

   b. Anthony invited a friend, Trisha, into his home. Trisha tripped over the dog and fell through a glass patio door and required medical treatment that cost $850. Anthony gave written notice to his insurer of the occurrence the following morning. The insurer offered to pay Trisha's medical expenses under Coverage F—Medical Payments to Others.

c. An elderly friend of Mabel's, Esther, tripped on a loose board and fell down the front steps of Anthony's home. Esther broke her hip and was hospitalized for four months, incurring medical expenses of $15,000. Anthony gave written notice to his insurer of the occurrence the following day. Before Esther's treatment was completed, Anthony filed for bankruptcy. The insurer offered to pay Esther's medical expenses under Coverage F—Medical Payments to Others up to the coverage limit.

Educational Objective 4
Summarize each of the HO-3 policy provisions in Sections I and II—Conditions.

Key Words and Phrases
Waiver

Apparent authority

Binding authority

First-party claim

Hold-harmless agreement

Review Questions

4-1. Identify the insured homeowners affected by the liberalization clause.

4-2. Explain why courts have permitted use of oral waivers by claim representatives made during the adjustment of a loss and after issuance of the written policy.

4-3. How is a conflict between policy language and state laws resolved when determining whether an insurer can cancel or nonrenew a policy?

4-4. Name a circumstance when an insurer might exercise its subrogation rights under a homeowners policy.

Application Question

4-5. One month after renewing their homeowners insurance policy, a married couple, Charlotte and Allan, sold their home to another married couple, Laura and Luke, who had just relocated from across the country. To make life a little easier for Laura and Luke, Charlotte and Allan decided to transfer their homeowners insurance to them. Explain whether this transfer is legally enforceable.

Educational Objective 5

Given a case describing a homeowners liability claim, determine whether the HO-3 Policy Section II—Liability Coverages would cover the claim, and, if so, the amount the insurer would pay for the claim.

Application Questions

The student should assume that all the case facts remain the same as those in the HO-3 Policy Section II—Liability Coverages case study unless a question states otherwise. The student also should refer to the policy language provided in the case study's exhibits to answer a question.

5-1. Two years after being bitten by Roberta and George's dog, Oliver developed a serious infection at the wound site due to a missed stitch. His additional medical expenses amounted to $650. Explain whether Oliver's medical expenses would be covered under Coverage F—Medical Payments to Others.

5-2. Roberta's nephew lives with her family. Suppose he broke the neighbor's sliding glass door's window. Explain whether the cost to replace the glass would be covered and, if so, under which coverage part.

5-3. What policy conditions would Oliver be required to comply with in order for his medical bills to be covered under Roberta and George's HO-3 policy?

Answers to Assignment 6 Questions

NOTE: These answers are provided to give students a basic understanding of acceptable types of responses. They often are not the only valid answers and are not intended to provide an exhaustive response to the questions.

Educational Objective 1

1-1. The HO-3 Section II Coverage E general coverage provisions provide coverage if a claim is made or a suit is brought against an insured because of bodily injury or property damage arising from a covered occurrence. Defense costs for any personal liability claim or suit are paid in addition to the limit of liability.

1-2. Under Coverage E, the insurer pays up to the limit of liability for the damages for which an insured is legally liable.

1-3. For defense cost coverage under Coverage E, the insured does not have to be found liable for damages because coverage is provided even if a suit is groundless, false, or fraudulent.

1-4. The insurer's obligation to defend an insured under Coverage E ends only when the liability limit for the occurrence is exhausted by payment of a settlement or judgment.

1-5. Coverage F provides coverage for medical payments incurred by others (not an insured or regular household residents) within three years of an injury. Medical expenses include reasonable charges for medical, surgical, X-ray, dental, ambulance, hospital, professional nursing, funeral services, and prosthetic devices up to a limit of $1,000 per person for a single accident.

1-6. Coverage E applies only when an insured is found legally responsible for damages. Under Coverage F, the need to determine whether an insured was legally responsible for the injuries is eliminated. Coverage F applies regardless of the insured's liability and claims for medical payments are often paid when the insured feels a moral obligation to another person.

1-7. These Additional Coverage expenses may be paid on the insured's behalf:
- Expenses the insurer incurs
- Premiums on bonds
- Reasonable expenses
- Postjudgment interest

1-8. The Damage to Property of Others additional coverage pays up to $1,000 for damage to property of others caused by an insured, regardless of fault or legal liability. This coverage will not pay for property damage to the extent of any amount recoverable under Section I of the policy.

1-9. a. Richard's HO-3 Section II Coverage F would provide $1,000 medical payments coverage for the girl's injuries. Coverage E would provide liability coverage for the girl's injuries and damages, assuming Richard is legally liable. Richard could be found negligent and, therefore, liable for the injury because the dog often escaped its fence and Richard had not corrected the situation. If the neighbors sued Richard, Coverage E would pay his defense costs until the liability limit for the occurrence is exhausted by payment of a settlement or judgment. The Section II—Additional Coverages would provide certain specified claim expenses related to any lawsuit that ensued in addition to any judgment or settlement.

b. Richard's Coverage F would pay the $700 in medical expenses because Tommy was an invited guest and the injury was accidental. Because Tommy was responsible for his own injury and Richard was supervising the children when the accident occurred, he would probably not be liable for the damages and Coverage E would not apply. However, the Section II—Additional Coverages would reimburse Richard for the first-aid supplies he used and the provision for damage to the property of others would pay the $300 to replace Tommy's broken glasses, avoiding any potential litigation expense to determine fault.

c. The Loss Assessment provision under Section II—Additional Coverages would pay $1,000 for Richard's share of the loss assessment.

d. Richard's Coverage E will pay for the property damage to his brother's golf cart. Coverage F will pay up to $1,000 for Sam's medical expenses and if they exceeded that amount, Coverage E will pay the medical expenses.

Educational Objective 2

2-1. The motor vehicle liability exclusion in HO-3 Section II is intended to exclude exposures covered by the Personal Auto Policy (PAP); however, certain motor vehicles specifically related to personal, residential use are covered by the HO-3 under an exception.

2-2. The exclusion of watercraft liability under HO-3 Section II includes these criteria in addition to organized racing events:
- The watercraft is rented to others.
- The watercraft is used to carry persons or cargo for a charge.
- The watercraft is used for any business purpose.

2-3. The exception applies to the Section II exclusion because the definition of an aircraft under the HO-3 policy excludes model airplanes and hobby aircraft that do not carry people or cargo.

2-4. If an insured intentionally causes or expects to cause bodily injury or property damage, then that injury or damage is excluded under Coverages E and F through the Expected or Intended Injury exclusion, even if the actual injury or damage that results was not intended.

2-5. The HO-3 Coverage E and F Business exclusion makes an exception for occasional and part-time business activities

2-6. If the vacation home was acquired by the insured before the insured's primary homeowners current policy period and the vacation home was not listed on the policy, the Insured's Premises Not an Insured Location exclusion would apply to the guest's injury that occurred at the vacation home.

2-7. Herpes, AIDS, and a common cold are three examples of communicable diseases that are excluded from liability under Coverages E and F.

2-8. The liability coverage under the HO-3 would not apply because Coverages E and F exclude coverage for any loss that arises out of mental abuse under the Sexual Molestation, Corporal Punishment, or Physical or Mental Abuse exclusion.

2-9. The HO-3 liability coverage would not apply because Coverages E and F exclude coverage for any loss that results from the use of controlled substances as defined by the Federal Food and Drug Law.

2-10. Coverage E excludes coverage for liability assessments charged to the policyholders; however, Section II—Additional Coverage provides $1,000 coverage for this exposure. Consequently, $1,000 of such losses would be covered under the HO-3.

2-11. Personal liability coverages under Coverage E are intended to address third-party liability loss exposures; therefore coverage is not provided if an insured damages his or her own property.

2-12. When a state law requires workers compensation benefits, the Coverage E Bodily Injury to Persons Eligible for Workers Compensation Benefits exclusion would apply to injuries of a domestic worker. Coverage for the domestic worker's injuries would not be provided under the HO-3 in this state.

2-13. a. The Coverage E and F Business exclusion could be considered; however, liability for rental as a private garage is an exception to the exclusion, so coverage is provided.

b. The Coverage E and F Business exclusion should be considered; however, coverage is available for an insured under the age of twenty-one involved in a part-time or occasional, self-employed business with no employees. Assuming Stacy has no employees, liability coverage would be provided.

c. The Coverage E and F Professional Services exclusion should be considered. The exclusion would apply to Paula's tax preparation business for which her liability should be covered under a professional liability policy. Therefore no coverage would apply under the HO-3 policy.

d. The Coverage E Damage to Property in the Insured's Care exclusion should be considered; however, the exception for property damage caused by fire, smoke, or explosion would apply. Terry and Paula's liability coverage would be provided for the damage to the friend's cabin because it was occupied by the insured when the damage occurred. For Stacy's injuries, both the Bodily Injury to an Insured exclusion and the Injury to Residence exclusion should be considered. These provisions would exclude liability coverage because Stacy was a resident relative (and thus an insured) under the age of twenty-one and in the insured's care when the injury occurred. The latter exclusion would apply even if Stacy was not a relative because she lived in the insured residence.

e. Both the Coverage F—Residence Employee Off Premises exclusion and the Bodily Injury Eligible for Workers Compensation Benefits exclusion could be considered. Because Holly was a residence employee who was off duty and away from the residence, the first exclusion would apply and coverage would not be provided. Although Holly was eligible to receive workers compensation benefits, those benefit would not accrue during her off-duty hours away from the residence premises, so the Bodily Injury Eligible for Workers Compensation Benefits exclusion would not apply in this situation and would not affect the Residence Employee Off Premises exclusion.

Educational Objective 3

3-1. The HO-3 Section II Limit of Liability condition specifies that the Coverage E limit does not increase regardless of the number of insureds, claims made, or people injured. The Limit of Liability condition also specifies that the Coverage F limit shown on the Declarations page is available for each person injured in one accident (occurrence).

3-2. The Severability of Insurance condition of the HO-3 specifies that each insured seeking protection is treated as if he or she has separate coverage under the policy. However, the insurer's limit of liability stated in the policy is not increased for any one occurrence if more than one insured is involved.

3-3. The insured's duties after an occurrence include these requirements:
- Give written notice
- Cooperate with the insurer
- Forward legal documents
- Provide claims assistance
- Submit evidence for damage to property of others
- Not make voluntary payments

3-4. The Duties of an Injured Person condition under Coverage F stipulates that, if an individual makes a claim for medical payments, three requirements must be met. The injured person (or someone acting on his or her behalf) must give the insurer written proof of the claim (under oath) as soon as possible and authorize the insurer to obtain copies of medical reports and records, and the injured person must submit to a physical exam by a doctor chosen by the insurer as often as the insurer requires such examinations.

3-5. The Coverage F Payment of Claim condition stipulates that the insurer's payment of a Medical Payments to Others claim is not an admission of liability by the insured or the insurer. Medical Payments coverage is intended to reduce the possibility of damages resulting from claims by providing prompt payment for the injured parties' medical expenses without the need to determine fault.

3-6. The Suit Against Us condition states that no action with respect to Coverage E can be brought against the insurer until the obligation of the insured has been determined by a final judgment or agreement signed by the insurer.

3-7. The Other Insurance condition for Coverage E stipulates that the Coverage E limits applicable to any occurrence are paid as excess over any other collectible insurance unless the other insurance is written specifically to provide excess coverage.

3-8. Under the Section II Concealment or Fraud condition, only the insured(s) involved in the concealment or fraud, or those making false statements, are excluded from liability coverage under the policy. Coverage would be provided for an innocent insured who was not involved.

3-9. a. Two conditions could affect coverage under the Section II Coverage E of Anthony's policy, the Duties After "Occurrence" and the Severability of Insurance conditions. Because Mabel is an insured, coverage is provided under the policy for her liability. Mabel complied with the conditions specified for Duties After "Occurrence," so coverage would be provided for Mabel's liability of $12,000 up to the policy limits. But Anthony did not comply with the duties, which hindered the insurer in performing its duties. Consequently, the insurer is not obligated to pay Anthony's liability under the policy. The Severability of Insurance condition allows Mabel to be treated as if she has separate coverage under the policy, so the insurer's denial of payment for Anthony's liability would not affect its payment of Mabel's liability. Anthony would be held personally responsible for the $8,000 liability settlement against him. Finally, the Suit Against Us condition could bar Anthony from suing his insurer because he failed to meet all of his obligations under Section II of the policy.

b. To obtain medical payments coverage, Trisha must comply with all requirements under the Duties of an Injured Person condition of Coverage F. The Payment of Claim condition would also apply to stipulate that the insurer's payment of Trisha's Medical Payments to Others claim is not an admission of liability for the occurrence. Anthony complied with the Duties After "Occurrence" condition so coverage was provided.

c. Because Anthony complied with the Duties After "Occurrence" condition, coverage would be available under the policy. To obtain Medical Payments coverage, Esther must comply with the Duties of an Injured Person condition of Coverage F, and the Payment of Claim condition would specify that the payment was not an admission of liability. Even though Anthony filed bankruptcy, the Bankruptcy of an Insured condition still obligated the insurer to pay Esther's bodily injury claim under Coverage E—Personal Liability.

Educational Objective 4

4-1. Only homeowners with the same edition of a policy that is subsequently changed by the insurer are affected by the liberalization clause, which specifies how broadened coverage applies to the policy.

4-2. Courts have recognized oral waivers by claim representatives made during the adjustment of a loss and after issuance of the written policy because claim representatives are the insurer's representatives and have apparent authority to modify policy conditions. As the insurer's agents, insurance agents with binding authority also are authorized to make policy changes through an oral binder that is effective until a written policy change endorsement is produced.

4-3. Because state law often dictates how and when insurers can cancel and nonrenew policies, whenever policy language and state laws conflict, state law takes precedence and overrides policy language.

4-4. An insurer might exercise its subrogation rights when it pays a claim for a covered property or liability loss caused by the negligence of another party.

4-5. Charlotte and Allan's transfer of their homeowners policy to Laura and Luke is not legally enforceable, because an insurance policy is a personal contract between the insurer and the policyholder. Therefore, the insurer must be able to choose whom it will insure. The assignment condition states that any assignment of the policy without the insurer's written consent is invalid. If an insured property is sold or otherwise transferred to another person, the new owner must qualify for a homeowners policy, even if the policy is intended to cover the same transferred property. Therefore, Laura and Luke must purchase their own policy.

Educational Objective 5

5-1. Oliver's medical expenses would be covered under Coverage F—Medical Payments to Others because Roberta and George's liability insurance will pay for Oliver's medical expenses up to three years after the date of the accident and up to the Coverage F limit of $5,000.

5-2. The cost to replace the glass would be covered because Section II—Additional Coverages includes residents of a household who are relatives of the named insured as insureds. Therefore, Roberta's nephew is considered an insured, and the cost to replace the sliding door's glass would be covered.

5-3. The conditions under which Oliver must comply include notifying the insurer of the loss and assisting the insurer as requested. For Section F—Medical Payments, Oliver is required to provide the insurer with written proof of loss and to authorize the insurer to obtain copies of any medical reports. Additionally, Oliver may be required to submit to a physical exam if requested by the insurer.

Direct Your Learning

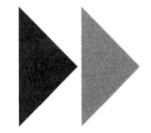

Assignment 7

Homeowners Coverage Forms and Endorsements

Educational Objectives

After learning the content of this assignment, you should be able to:

1. Compare the coverage provided by each of the following homeowners policies to the coverage provided by the HO-3 policy:
   - HO-2—Broad Form
   - HO-5—Comprehensive Form
   - HO-4—Contents Broad Form
   - HO-6—Unit-Owners Form
   - HO-8—Modified Coverage Form

2. Summarize the coverages provided by various ISO homeowners policy endorsements.

3. Given a case describing a homeowners claim, determine whether an HO-3 Policy (endorsed or unendorsed) would cover the claim, and if so, the amount the insurer would pay for the claim.

Study Materials

Required Reading:
- Personal Insurance
  - Chapter 7

Study Aids:
- SMART Online Practice Exams
- SMART Study Aids
  - Review Notes and Flash Cards—Assignment 7

Outline

- **Variations in ISO Homeowners Forms**
  - A. HO-2 Broad Form Compared With HO-3
  - B. HO-5 Comprehensive Form Compared With HO-3
  - C. HO-4 Contents Broad Form Compared With HO-3
  - D. HO-6 Unit-Owners Form Compared With HO-3
  - E. HO-8 Modified Coverage Form Compared With HO-3
- **Common Endorsements That Modify ISO Homeowners Policies**
  - A. Inflation Guard Endorsement
  - B. Scheduled Personal Property Endorsement
  - C. Personal Property Replacement Cost Loss Settlement Endorsement
  - D. Personal Injury Endorsement
  - E. Home Business Insurance Coverage Endorsement (HOMEBIZ)
  - F. Earthquake Endorsement
  - G. Ordinance or Law—Increased Amount of Coverage Endorsement
  - H. Water Back Up and Sump Discharge or Overflow Endorsement
  - I. Loss Assessment Coverage
  - J. Additional Residence Rented to Others—1, 2, 3, or 4 Families Endorsement
  - K. Credit Card, Electronic Fund Transfer Card or Access Device, Forgery and Counterfeit Money Coverage—Increased Limit Endorsement
  - L. Limited Fungi, Wet or Dry Rot, or Bacteria Coverage Endorsement
- **HO-3 (Endorsed or Unendorsed) Coverage Case**
  - A. Case Facts
  - B. Case Analysis Tools
  - C. Determination of Coverage
  - D. Determination of Amounts Payable
- **Summary**

For each assignment, you should define or describe each of the Key Words and Phrases and answer each of the Review and Application Questions.

Educational Objective 1
Compare the coverage provided by each of the following homeowners policies to the coverage provided by the HO-3 policy:
- HO-2—Broad Form
- HO-5—Comprehensive Form
- HO-4—Contents Broad Form
- HO-6—Unit-Owners Form
- HO-8—Modified Coverage Form

Key Words and Phrases

Named peril

Burden of proof

Condominium, or cooperative unit

Moral hazard

Review Questions

1-1. What are the primary differences between the HO-3 policy form and the other homeowners forms?

1-2. Both the HO-2 and HO-3 policy forms are designed for owner-occupants of a house. Why might a homeowner choose to use the HO-2 policy form instead of the HO-3?

1-3. How does the burden of proof relating to losses under named perils coverages differ from the burden of proof relating to losses under special forms coverages?

1-4. How does Coverage C—Personal Property differ in the HO-3 and HO-5 policies?

Application Question

1-5. Jim and Ann purchased a home at a bargain price. The home has many unique features that include carved wood doors, a spiral staircase, and antique light fixtures that would be expensive to replace if the home sustained major damage. Which homeowners policy would be appropriate for the loss exposures for this home?

Educational Objective 2
Summarize the coverages provided by various ISO homeowners policy endorsements.

Key Word or Phrase
Scheduled coverage

Review Questions

2-1. Describe how the homeowners policy Inflation Guard endorsement operates.

2-2. When the Personal Property Replacement Cost Loss Settlement endorsement is added to a homeowners policy, why do many insurers require a higher than usual limit for Coverage C—Personal Property?

2-3. List the minimum eligibility requirements for a home business to expand coverage using the Home Business Insurance Coverage endorsement (HOMEBIZ).

2-4. Why might an insured choose to add the Credit Card, Electronic Fund Transfer Card or Access Device, Forgery and Counterfeit Money Coverage—Increased Limit endorsement to a homeowners policy, even though cardholders' liability is already limited by law and cardholder agreements?

Application Question

2-5. Paul and Deb recently built a new $250,000 home in Florida, which they have insured for $250,000 under a homeowners HO-3 policy. The home is located in an area where property values are expected to increase steadily over the next few years. Paul and Deb collect antiques, and Paul owns a coin collection that includes several rare coins. They have installed a home security system to protect their home from fire and theft.

Identify endorsements that Paul and Deb might decide to purchase to modify their HO-3 policy.

Educational Objective 3

Given a case describing a homeowners claim, determine whether an HO-3 Policy (endorsed or unendorsed) would cover the claim, and if so, the amount the insurer would pay for the claim.

Application Questions

The student should assume that all the case facts remain the same as those in the HO-3 Policy case study unless a question states otherwise. The student also should refer to the policy language provided in the case study's exhibits to answer a question.

3-1. While repairing her storm-damaged residence, Rochelle also decided to upgrade the plumbing in her bathroom (that was not storm damaged) to include new pipes and fixtures that would comply with a new building code. Determine whether the upgrade would be a covered expense in the Loss Settlement provisions of Rochelle's HO-3.

3-2. Suppose Rochelle furnished her investment property before Joe and Sandy moved in and that Rochelle's furniture was damaged from the broken windows during the storm. Determine whether her damaged furniture would be covered under Rochelle's homeowners policy and the endorsement that extends to the rental location.

3-3. Suppose damage to Rochelle's "Seaside Memories" business also included a computer, valued at $1,500, that she used exclusively in the business. The computer hardware was damaged in the storm. Determine whether Coverage C—Personal Property coverage applies to the computer.

3-4. Suppose Rochelle's friend's boat and trailer, while in the insured's care, were damaged in an electrical fire (rather than a storm) at Rochelle's dwelling. Determine whether the fire peril would trigger liability coverage for property damaged (the fishing boat) while in Rochelle's care.

3-5. Joe and Sandy sued Rochelle for the $3,000 damage to their furniture and curtains. Explain how Rochelle's Section II coverage would protect her in this suit.

3-6. Suppose Rochelle had a $500 deductible on her HO-3 policy and that these amounts were the claim totals resulting from the storm damage and resulting liability:

Section I:	$80,000
Section II:	$4,000
HO 04 77 (Ordinance or Law Increased Amount of Coverage endorsement):	$5,000

Calculate the total claim paid under Rochelle's endorsed HO-3.

Answers to Assignment 7 Questions

NOTE: These answers are provided to give students a basic understanding of acceptable types of responses. They often are not the only valid answers and are not intended to provide an exhaustive response to the questions.

Educational Objective 1

1-1. The primary differences between the HO-3 policy form and the other homeowners forms are in Section I—Property Coverages of the various forms.

1-2. A homeowner might choose to use the HO-2 policy form instead of the HO-3 because the HO-2 limits causes of loss to the named perils listed in the policy and thus has a slightly lower premium.

1-3.
- With named perils coverage, the burden of proof is on the insured; that is, for coverage to apply, the insured must prove that the loss was caused by a covered cause of loss.
- With special form coverage, the burden of proof is on the insurer; that is, to deny coverage, the insurer must prove that the loss was caused by an excluded cause of loss.

1-4. These are differences between HO-3 Coverage C and HO-5 Coverage C:
- The HO-5 covers loss to personal property by any peril, including items that are misplaced or lost (subject to a dollar limit). The HO-3 does not cover such items.
- The HO-5 broadens personal property coverage by not excluding an exposure that has been excluded by the HO-3 policy.

1-5. An HO-8 policy would be a logical policy choice because replacement of the unique features, such as the light fixtures, due to a covered cause of loss, would likely exceed the market value of the house.

Educational Objective 2

2-1. The Inflation Guard endorsement gradually and automatically increases limits throughout the policy period for Coverages A, B, C, and D. Each year the insured and insurer agree on a percentage of increase that is applied to the original amount of insurance.

2-2. Many insurers require a higher Coverage C—Personal Property limit in a policy with the Personal Property Replacement Cost Loss Settlement endorsement because the value of property based on replacement cost is usually higher than the value of personal property based on actual value.

2-3. To be eligible for the HOMEBIZ endorsement, a home business must meet these minimum requirements:
- The business must be owned by an insured or a business entity comprising only the insured and resident relatives.
- It must be operated from the resident premises identified on the homeowners Dec page, and the resident premises is used primarily for residential purposes.
- It can have up to three employees.
- It cannot involve the manufacture, sale, or distribution of food products.
- It cannot involve the manufacture of personal care products.

- It cannot involve the sale or distribution of personal care products manufactured by the insured.
- It cannot have gross annual receipts exceeding $250,000.

2-4. An insured who holds numerous credit cards or who has large checking account balances subject to forgery might choose this endorsement because of the additional coverage—up to $10,000—it offers.

2-5. Paul and Deb might choose to purchase these endorsements to modify their HO-3 homeowners policy:
- Scheduled Personal Property Endorsement to provide scheduled coverage for their antiques and the coin collection
- Inflation Guard endorsement to automatically increase coverage limits as the property values increase in the area.

Educational Objective 3

3-1. Rochelle's HO-3 Loss Settlement provisions state that her insurer will pay the cost to repair or replace the part of the insured residence with material of like kind and quality as the dwelling had before the loss occurred. Because Rochelle's bathroom was unaffected by the storm, the upgraded plumbing would not be a covered expense.

3-2. Rochelle's investment property is only insured for liability. Section II Coverage E—Personal Liability does not apply to damage to property owned by an insured. Therefore, Rochelle's damaged furniture would not be covered under her endorsed homeowners policy.

3-3. Coverage C—Personal Property coverage has a Special Limit of Liability of $2,500 that applies to business property. Therefore, coverage applies to the computer loss up to $1,500. However, total Coverage C payments for business personal property (including the computer loss and any damaged inventory) cannot exceed the $2,500 Special Limit of Liability.

3-4. Coverage E excludes damage to property rented to, occupied, or used by or in the care of the insured. However, this exclusion does not apply to property damage caused by fire. Therefore, the damage to the fishing boat and trailer would be covered in Rochelle's HO-3.

3-5. Because Rochelle added liability coverage for her investment property to the HO-3 and because the damage to Joe and Sandy's furniture and curtains was caused by a covered occurrence, Rochelle's insurance would provide a defense against Joe and Sandy's suit.

3-6. The total paid claim under Rochelle's endorsed HO-3 equals $88,500. Note that the $500 deductible applicable to Rochelle's policy is applied only once to the total Homeowners Section I loss portion of $79,500 ($80,000 minus $500). The Section II amount payable is $4,000, and the additional amount payable under the endorsement is $5,000, for a total paid claim amount of $88,500.

Direct Your Learning

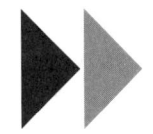

ASSIGNMENT 8

Other Residential Insurance

Educational Objectives

After learning the content of this assignment, you should be able to:

1. Contrast the DP-3 policy with the HO-3 policy in regard to each of the following:
   - Types of property covered
   - Other coverages
   - Perils insured against
   - Exclusions and conditions
   - Coverage for liability and theft losses

2. Given a case describing a dwelling claim, determine whether the DP-3 policy would cover the claim and, if so, the amount the insurer would pay for the claim.

3. Explain how the coverages under the HO-3 policy are modified by the Mobilehome Endorsement (MH 04 01) and other ISO endorsements unique to mobilehome coverage.

4. Describe the operation of the National Flood Insurance Program and the coverage it provides.

5. Describe the operation of FAIR plans and beachfront and windstorm plans and the coverage they provide.

Study Materials

Required Reading:
- Personal Insurance
  - Chapter 8

Study Aids:
- SMART Online Practice Exams
- SMART Study Aids
  - Review Notes and Flash Cards—Assignment 8

8.1

Outline

- **Dwelling Policies**
    - A. The ISO Dwelling Property 3—Special Form
    - B. Structures Eligible for Dwelling Policies
    - C. Coverages
        1. Coverage A—Dwelling
        2. Coverage B—Other Structures
        3. Coverage C—Personal Property
        4. Coverage D—Fair Rental Value and Coverage E—Additional Living Expense
    - D. Other Coverages
        1. Other Structures
        2. Debris Removal
        3. Improvements, Alterations, and Additions
        4. Worldwide Coverage
        5. Fair Rental Value and Additional Living Expense
        6. Reasonable Repairs
        7. Property Removed
        8. Trees, Shrubs, and Other Plants
        9. Fire Department Service Charge
        10. Collapse
        11. Glass or Safety Glazing Material
        12. Ordinance or Law
    - E. Perils Insured Against
    - F. Dwelling Policy General Exclusions
    - G. Dwelling Policy Conditions
    - H. Coverage for Liability and Theft Losses
        1. Personal Liability Supplement
        2. Residential Theft Coverage
- **Dwelling Coverage Case**
    - A. Case Facts
    - B. Case Analysis Tools
    - C. Determination of Coverage
    - D. Determination of Amounts Payable
- **Mobilehome Coverage**
    - A. Mobilehome Exposures
        1. Vulnerability to Additional Exposures
        2. Other Property Exposure Considerations
    - B. Mobilehome Coverages
        1. ISO Mobilehome Endorsement
    - C. Other ISO Mobilehome Endorsements
- **The National Flood Insurance Program**
    - A. Community Eligibility
    - B. Incentives
        1. Emergency Program
        2. Regular Program
    - C. Flood Insurance Coverage
        1. Waiting Period
        2. Write-Your-Own (WYO) Program
    - D. Flood Insurance Reform
- **FAIR and Beachfront and Windstorm Plans**
    - A. FAIR Plans
        1. Purpose and Operation
        2. Eligible Property
        3. Coverages
    - B. Beachfront and Windstorm Plans
        1. Purpose and Operation
        2. Eligible Property
        3. Coverages
- **Summary**

Study tips: Plan to register with the Institutes well in advance of your exam. Please consult the registration booklet that accompanied this course guide for complete information regarding exam dates and fees.

For each assignment, you should define or describe each of the Key Words and Phrases and answer each of the Review and Application Questions.

> ## Educational Objective 1
> Contrast the DP-3 policy with the HO-3 policy in regard to each of the following:
> - Types of property covered
> - Other coverages
> - Perils insured against
> - Exclusions and conditions
> - Coverage for liability and theft losses

Review Questions

1-1. Under what circumstances would an applicant purchase a dwelling policy rather than a homeowners policy to insure a residence?

1-2. What is the most important difference between an unendorsed DP-3 policy and a homeowners policy?

1-3. Identify the structures that are eligible for dwelling policies.

1-4. How does the availability of property coverages under the dwelling policy differ from the availability of property coverages under the homeowners policy?

1-5. How does Coverage A—Dwelling coverage under the DP-3 differ from that coverage under the HO-3?

1-6. How are gravemarkers and mausoleums treated differently under the DP-3 Coverage B—Other Structures compared with treatment of such property under the HO-3?

1-7. Under the DP-3, when Coverage C—Personal Property is selected and specified with a limit on the Declarations page, how does the coverage differ from property covered under special limits of liability in Coverage C of the HO-3?

1-8. How does Coverage D—Fair Rental Value and Coverage E—Additional Living Expenses under the DP-3 compare to comparable coverages under the HO-3?

1-9. Explain how each of these Other Coverages under the DP-3 differ from any comparable coverages under the HO-3:

a. Other Structures

b. Improvements, Alterations, and Additions

c. Worldwide Coverage

d. Fair Rental Value and Additional Living Expense

e. Ordinance or Law

1-10. How do the perils insured against under the DP-3 Coverages A and B differ from the perils insured against for those coverages under the HO-3?

1-11. Explain how the general exclusions under the DP-3 compare to the HO-3 Section I exclusions.

1-12. Explain the options for insureds who purchase dwelling policies and wish to add coverage for personal liability.

1-13. Identify the two residential theft endorsements from which an insured may choose to add theft coverage to a dwelling policy and explain the difference between them.

Application Question

1-14. Sally has a DP-3 policy to insure her rural dwelling and personal property. Limits for Coverages A through E are listed on her Declarations page and she paid the appropriate premium. She purchased no additional endorsements. For each of these situations, explain whether coverage would be provided and, if so, identify the applicable coverage(s):

   a. Sally's toaster malfunctioned and caused a fire in her kitchen while she was working outside. Before the fire department from the neighboring city could respond, her kitchen and appliances sustained extensive damage from the fire and smoke. Silverware, dishes, $500 cash, and other items of personal property in the kitchen were destroyed. The remainder of the dwelling sustained smoke damage. Sally purchased a large heavy tarp to cover the damaged area of her roof to avoid further damage to the property. She was forced to rent an apartment until the damage was repaired.

   b. An invited guest to Sally's dwelling tripped on a rug in the hallway and fell, breaking his arm.

   c. While Sally was at work, her dwelling was broken into and someone stole her personal computer, her television, $3,000 worth of jewelry, and $1,000 in cash and bank notes.

d. Sally returned from work one day to find her storm door shattered and a hole in the etched-glass window of her front door. She found a rock lying amongst the glass shards on her living room floor.

e. One afternoon, Sally's sewer backed up while she was doing laundry because of tree roots that had grown into the drain and caused a blockage. Her basement carpet in the adjoining room was damaged by the backup of sewer water.

Educational Objective 2
Given a case describing a dwelling claim, determine whether the DP-3 policy would cover the claim and, if so, the amount the insurer would pay for the claim.

Review Questions

2-1. How would Wally and Dawn's claim payment be affected if their DP-3 policy had included a theft endorsement?

2-2. Suppose Wally and Dawn's property was adjacent to a factory that emitted smoke from its smokestacks, damaging Wally and Dawn's furniture. Would Wally and Dawn's DP-3 cover the cost to replace the damaged furniture?

2-3. Suppose Wally and Dawn's home repairs were completed on June 15, but they stayed in the rented apartment until July 15. Explain how Wally and Dawn's insurer would handle their additional living expenses for that period.

Educational Objective 3

Explain how the coverages under the HO-3 policy are modified by the Mobilehome Endorsement (MH 04 01) and other ISO endorsements unique to mobilehome coverage.

Review Questions

3-1. Identify three exposures to loss faced by owners of mobilehomes that are similar to exposures faced by owners of conventional homes.

3-2. To what additional exposures are mobilehomes vulnerable because of their construction? Explain your answer.

3-3. How does the use of mobilehomes as vacation homes affect their vulnerability to additional exposures?

3-4. Why is the distinction between the dwelling coverage and personal property coverage a special consideration for mobilehomes?

3-5. Describe each of these modifications to the HO-3 policy that results from adding a Mobilehome Endorsement and a declarations page to create a mobilehome policy:

a. Definition of "residence premises"

b. Coverage A property

c. "Property removed" coverage

d. Coverage for repair or replacement of panels

3-6. Describe each of these additional mobilehome endorsements.

a. Actual Cash Value Mobilehome endorsement

b. Transportation/Permission to Move endorsement

c. Mobilehome Lienholder's Single Interest endorsement

Application Question

3-7. Jake wants to insure his mobilehome with a mobilehome policy. The mobilehome, which is permanently anchored in its wooded, secluded location, meets the insurer's requirements for coverage. For these exposures, what coverage would be provided in the mobilehome policy/endorsement and the additional available endorsements?

a. High winds are common in this area and could threaten the entire structure or panels on the mobilehome. Temporary removal of the mobilehome offers Jake an option to avoid or reduce the damage.

b. Jake's lienholder is concerned about its interest in the mobilehome above Jake's interests. It is concerned about transportation perils and any ordinances that might alter its right to the mobilehome as collateral. In accordance with its business policies, the lienholder requires coverage to protect it from this possibility.

Educational Objective 4
Describe the operation of the National Flood Insurance Program and the coverage it provides.

Key Words and Phrases

Flood

Special flood hazard area (SFHA)

Flood hazard boundary map

Emergency program

Flood Insurance Rate Map (FIRM)

Regular program

Adverse selection

Write-Your-Own (WYO) program

Review Questions

4-1. Describe the two ways a community's residents become eligible for flood insurance under the National Flood Insurance Program (NFIP).

4-2. Describe the assistance available to special flood hazard area (SFHA) residents not participating in the NFIP if disaster occurs as a result of flooding in a community, and any special restrictions on assistance.

4-3. Describe the insurance property owners can purchase when a community first joins the NFIP and the actions the FIA takes when a community first joins the NFIP.

4-4. Describe the three federal flood insurance policies available to insureds.

4-5. How long is the waiting period required by the NFIP, and why is it required?

4-6. Describe the exception to the NFIP's waiting period.

4-7. Describe the roles of the FIA, NFIP, and an insurer participating in the Write-Your-Own (WYO) program.

Application Question

4-8. Karen purchased a home for $250,000 in a community that is eligible for flood insurance under the NFIP emergency program. Karen's home is in a special flood hazard area. What incentive does Karen have to encourage her community to enter the NFIP regular program as soon as possible?

Educational Objective 5
Describe the operation of FAIR plans and beachfront and windstorm plans and the coverage they provide.

Key Words and Phrases
Syndicate

Difference in conditions policy (DIC)

Review Questions

5-1. What is the purpose of a Fair Access to Insurance Requirements (FAIR) plan (or a beachfront and windstorm plan)?

5-2. Describe three types of loss exposures that resulted in the creation of FAIR plans.

5-3. Explain how FAIR plans provide insurance, service policies, and fund losses paid under the plan.

5-4. If a FAIR plan administrator finds that a property fails to meet the basic safety levels, can the owner obtain coverage under a state FAIR plan? Explain your answer.

5-5. What four coverages are usually available under FAIR plans?

5-6. Describe the various operations of beachfront and windstorm plans.

5-7. What requirements do states have for properties to be eligible for coverage under beachfront and windstorm plans?

5-8. What are the two primary perils insured against under beachfront and windstorm plans?

5-9. What special provision under beachfront and windstorm plans might restrict applications for new coverage and/or increases in limits?

Application Question

5-10. Sarah wishes to purchase an expensive home in a suburb that is located near a heavily wooded area. Because of the increased fire hazard, she is unable to obtain insurance for the property. The financing organization requires insurance coverage and recommends that Sarah apply for coverage under the state FAIR plan.

   a. What must Sarah do for her otherwise uninsurable property to be eligible under the FAIR plan?

   b. Because Sarah's state FAIR plan provides only fire, vandalism, riot, and windstorm coverages, and the financing organization requires coverage against all common homeowners perils, what action should Sarah take to obtain the needed coverage? Explain your answer.

Answers to Assignment 8 Questions

NOTE: These answers are provided to give students a basic understanding of acceptable types of responses. They often are not the only valid answers and are not intended to provide an exhaustive response to the questions.

Educational Objective 1

1-1. An applicant would purchase a dwelling policy rather than a homeowners policy if the residence is not eligible for homeowners coverage because it is not owner-occupied, the dwelling is below the minimum limit, or the residence does not meet other insurer's underwriting guidelines. Also, some insureds do not want or need the full range of homeowners coverages, and a homeowners policy might cost more than the insured is willing to pay.

1-2. The most important difference between an unendorsed DP-3 policy and a homeowners policy is that, unlike most homeowners policies, an unendorsed DP-3 does not provide any theft coverage for personal property or any liability coverages.

1-3. Structures eligible for dwelling policies include these:
- Owner-occupied or tenant-occupied one- to four-family dwellings
- A dwelling in the course of construction
- Mobilehomes at a permanent location
- Houseboats, in some states
- Certain incidental business occupancies, if the businesses are operated by the owner-insured or by a tenant of the insured location

1-4. The same property coverages can apply under the dwelling policy that are included under the homeowners policy; however, under the dwelling policy, each desired coverage must be listed with a limit on the declarations page for the coverage to apply. In contrast, under the homeowners policy, all of these coverages apply automatically.

1-5. The DP-3 form specifies that coverage is provided for the dwelling on the location described in the declarations and specifies that it must be used principally for dwelling purposes. In contrast, the HO-3 refers to the dwelling on the residence premises, including attached structures. The DP-3 also states that coverage is provided for building and outdoor equipment used for the service of the premises and located on the described location, unless it is covered elsewhere in the policy. While the HO-3 covers this property, it is covered under Coverage C—Personal Property.

1-6. Under the DP-3 Coverage B, gravemarkers and mausoleums are specifically excluded. In contrast, the HO-3 Additional Coverage provides up to $5,000 for gravemarkers.

1-7. The HO-3 Coverage C specifies special limits that apply to specific types of personal property. Because the perils and some coverages differ under the DP-3 policy, these limits are not necessary; therefore no specified limits apply for specific types of property.

1-8. Coverages D and E in the DP-3 form correspond roughly to Coverage D—Loss of Use in the HO-3 form (which essentially provides coverage for both). Coverage D covers the fair rental value of a property rented to others when it becomes unfit for normal use because of a covered loss. Coverage E covers the increase in living expenses when the described property becomes unfit for normal use because of a covered loss.

1-9. a. Under the Other Coverages provision, the DP-3 form provides up to 10 percent of the Coverage A limit for Coverage B—Other Structures. This additional insurance amount does not reduce the Coverage A limit for the same loss.

b. The DP-3 form provides 10 percent of the Coverage C limit as additional insurance to cover a tenant's improvements, alterations, and additions for a covered loss. The HO-3 has no comparable coverage.

c. The DP-3 form provides up to 10 percent of the Coverage C limit for loss to the Coverage C property anywhere in the world (as does the HO-3 Coverage C), except that the DP-3 Coverage C excludes rowboats and canoes. Additionally, the HO-3 Coverage C limits the coverage for property that is usually located at a secondary residence of the insured to 10 percent.

d. The DP-3 form provides up to 20 percent of the Coverage A limit for losses under both Coverages D and E. In contrast, under the HO-3 form, the corresponding additional limit for loss of use is 30 percent of the Coverage A limit.

e. The DP-3 form provides coverage for increased costs the insured incurs because of the enforcement of any ordinance or law. If the insured purchased Coverage A, ordinance or law coverage is 10 percent of the Coverage A limit. If no Coverage A limit exists, then up to 10 percent of the Coverage B limit is provided for ordinance or law coverage. In contrast, the HO-3 form provides up to 10 percent of Coverage A for ordinance and law coverage as an additional coverage. Under the DP-3, if the insured is a tenant, the 10 percent limit applies to improvements, alternations, and additions.

1-10. The DP-3 and the HO-3 approach the perils insured against in the same manner (using a special form approach in which excluded perils are not covered); however, more perils are excluded under the DP-3, such as theft of property that is not part of a covered building or structure and wind, hail, ice, snow, or sleet that damage specific types of property.

1-11. The general exclusions in the DP-3 closely resemble the HO-3 Section I exclusions including loss caused directly or indirectly by several specified perils or events. These perils and events are essentially the same in both policies.

1-12. Insureds who purchase dwelling policies can add a personal liability supplement, either written as an addendum to the dwelling policy or as a separate policy using the personal liability supplement. If an insured has both a homeowners policy on a residence and a dwelling policy on a rental dwelling, then that insured can purchase a homeowners additional residence rented to other endorsement to cover the liability for the rented dwelling.

1-13. The Broad Theft Coverage endorsement provides coverage against the perils of theft, including attempted theft, and vandalism or malicious mischief as a result of theft or attempted theft on-premises and off-premises (available if on-premises coverage is purchased). The endorsement specifies special limits. The Limited Theft Coverage endorsement covers the same perils as the other theft endorsement, but only applies on-premises. This endorsement includes special limits only for watercraft and their trailers, trailers not used for watercraft, and firearms and related equipment.

1-14. a. Sally's property damage to the kitchen and other parts of the dwelling would be covered under her DP-3 policy, Coverage A—Dwelling up to the limits specified in the Declarations page. Except for the $500 cash (money is excluded), her personal property including the silverware and dishes would be covered under Coverage C—Personal Property on an actual cash value (ACV) basis up to the limits specified in the Declarations page. The DP-3 other coverage for reasonable repairs would cover the cost of the tarp that Sally purchased and any cost to attach it to the roof (if within the Coverage A limit), and the fire department service charge would be covered up to $500. Coverage E—Additional Living Expense would apply to her rental expense while the damage was repaired, up to the applicable limit.

b. Sally's unendorsed DP-3 policy does not provide any liability coverage. Therefore, no coverage would be provided for the guest's injuries.

c. Sally's unendorsed DP-3 policy does not provide any coverage for personal property theft losses. Therefore, no coverage would be provided for the computer, television, jewelry, cash, or bank notes. However, Coverage A would pay for any damage to the dwelling caused by the burglar.

d. The other coverage for glass or safety glazing material under Sally's DP-3 policy would pay to replace the storm door and the glass in the front door.

e. A general exclusion under the DP-3 excludes water damage such as that caused by flood and backup of sewers and drains. Therefore, Sally's DP-3 would provide no coverage for the damaged carpet.

Educational Objective 2

2-1. If Wally and Dawn's DP-3 policy had included a theft endorsement, the loss of their television and stereo equipment would be covered, increasing their claim payment by $2,800 (the ACV of the stolen items).

2-2. The damage to Wally and Dawn's furniture would not be covered under their DP-3 because smoke from agricultural smudging or industrial operations is excluded in Coverage C—Personal Property.

2-3. The insurer would cover the couple's additional living expenses only until June 15, when their home became habitable. Wally and Dawn would be responsible for their additional living expenses after June 15.

Educational Objective 3

3-1. Owners of mobilehomes face loss exposures similar to those faced by owners of conventional homes, including these (any three):
- Damage to or destruction of the mobilehome
- Damage to or destruction of other structures on the residence premises
- Damage to or destruction of personal property in the mobilehome or in other structures
- Loss of use of the mobilehome
- Liability loss because of bodily injury to others or damage to the property of others

3-2. The construction materials and loose foundation of mobilehomes make them vulnerable to additional exposures. Mobilehomes are constructed of lighter materials than those used for homes built on permanent foundations, and special construction techniques are used. A mobilehome's wheels are generally removed, and the structure is set on blocks, piers, or masonry footings. A mobilehome without protective skirting attached to the bottom is vulnerable to a buildup of debris underneath it that may result in damage.

3-3. The use of mobilehomes as vacation homes can affect their vulnerability to additional exposures because they may be located in recreational areas or areas subject to greater loss exposure, such as in the mountains, beside a lake or river, or in heavily wooded areas. The absence of services, such as fire and telephone services, and the absence of nearby neighbors (who could report a fire) can increase the severity if a loss occurs.

3-4. Certain contents in mobilehomes, such as built-in cabinets, appliances, and furniture, are considered part of the mobilehome; in conventional homes, such contents may be considered personal property. This distinction determines whether dwelling or personal property coverage applies for such contents.

3-5.
  a. The definition of "residence premises" is changed in the Mobilehome Endorsement to mean the mobilehome and other structures located on land owned or leased by the insured where the insured resides at the location shown in the Declarations page.

  b. In the Mobilehome Endorsement, Coverage A—Dwelling is changed to apply to a mobilehome used primarily as a private residence and the structures and utility tanks attached to it. It also includes floor coverings, appliances, dressers, cabinets, and similar items that are permanently installed. Coverage is provided for materials and supplies for construction, alteration, or repair of the mobilehome or other structures on the premises.

  c. The Mobilehome Endorsement adds a unique "property removed" coverage that applies if the mobilehome is endangered by an insured peril, requiring removal to avoid damage. This coverage provides up to $500 for reasonable expenses incurred by the policyholder to remove and return the entire mobilehome.

  d. The Mobilehome Endorsement provides an additional coverage to repair or replace damaged parts of a series (not the entire series) of panels to match the remainder of the panels as closely as possible or to provide an acceptable decorative effect.

3-6.
  a. The Actual Cash Value Mobilehome endorsement changes the loss settlement terms on the mobilehome and other structures (including carpeting and appliances that are included as part of the mobilehome under Coverage A) to apply an actual cash value (ACV) basis rather than a replacement cost basis for losses.

  b. The Transportation/Permission to Move endorsement provides coverage for perils of transportation (collision, upset, stranding, or sinking) and coverage for the mobilehome and other structures at the new location anywhere in the United States or Canada for thirty days from the endorsement's effective date. A special deductible applies to this coverage.

  c. The Mobilehome Lienholder's Single Interest endorsement provides coverage only to a lienholder (on request) for collision and upset transportation exposures, subject to numerous recovery conditions. It also provides coverage to the lienholder for any loss resulting from the owner's conversion, embezzlement, or secretion of the mobilehome.

3-7.
  a. The mobilehome policy/endorsement provides coverage for this residence premises under Coverage A. The Additional Coverage under Section I provides up to $500 for Jake to remove the entire mobilehome from the threat of a pending severe storm and return it afterwards. Jake could increase that $500 limit by adding the Property Removed Increased Limit endorsement. The Loss to a Pair or Set Condition in Section I of the Mobilehome Endorsement would cover repair or replacement of any damaged panels on the mobilehome to match the remaining panels or provide an acceptable decorative effect.

b. The Mobilehome Endorsement and the declarations page in Jake's policy provide all coverages necessary to protect a listed lienholder because the endorsement modifies the word "mortgagee" to include a lienholder. The Transportation/Permission to Move endorsement covers most transportation perils and the Ordinance or Law Coverage endorsement returns coverage for ordinance or law exposures to the policy. The Mobilehome Lienholder's Single Interest endorsement would meet the lienholder's requirement for coverage against secretion and should resolve the lienholder's concerns about transportation perils because it provides coverage only to the lienholder.

Educational Objective 4

4-1. A community's residents become eligible for flood insurance under the NFIP in two ways:
- The community applies to the Federal Insurance Administration (FIA) to be included in the NFIP.
- The Federal Emergency Management Agency (FEMA) determines that an area is flood-prone and notifies the community that it has one year to decide whether to join the NFIP. A community that chooses not to join the NFIP is not eligible for federal flood assistance.

4-2. If a disaster occurs as a result of flooding in a nonparticipating community, no federal financial assistance can be provided for the permanent repair or reconstruction of insurable buildings in SFHAs. Eligible applicants for disaster assistance may, however, receive forms of disaster assistance that are not related to permanent repair and reconstruction of buildings. If a community is accepted into the NFIP within six months of a disaster, these limitations on federal disaster assistance are lifted.

4-3. When a community first joins the NFIP, property owners in special flood hazard areas can purchase limited amounts of insurance at subsidized rates under the initial phase of the program, called the emergency program. Although the community is eligible under the emergency program, the FIA arranges for a detailed study of the community and its susceptibility to flood. The study results in the publication of a Flood Insurance Rate Map (FIRM) that divides the community into specific zones to identify the probability of flooding in each zone.

4-4. Three federal flood insurance policies are available to insureds:
- The dwelling form is used for any dwelling having an occupancy of no more than four families, such as single-family homes, townhouses, row houses, and individual condominium units.
- The general property form is used for all other occupancies—that is, multi-residential and nonresidential, except for residential condominium building associations.
- Residential condominium building associations are eligible for coverage under the residential condominium building association form.

4-5. The NFIP generally requires a thirty-day waiting period for new flood insurance policies and for endorsements that increase coverage on existing policies. The waiting period prevents adverse selection.

4-6. An exception to the NFIP's waiting period is made for flood insurance that is purchased initially in connection with a property purchase or a new or an increased mortgage on a property. In such cases, the policy becomes effective at the time the property is transferred or the mortgage becomes effective, provided that the policy is applied for and the premium paid at or before the transfer of ownership or date of mortgage.

4-7. In the WYO program, the FIA determines rates, coverage limitations, and eligibility. Insurers collect premiums, retain commissions, and use the remainder of the premiums to pay claims. Insurers receive an expense allowance for policies written and claims processed, while the federal government retains responsibility for losses. The NFIP totally reinsures the coverage.

4-8. While the community is in the emergency flood insurance program, only $35,000 in flood insurance is available. If the community complies with the flood control and land-use restrictions required by the NFIP, and the maps are created for the specific flood zones, the community may change to the regular flood program. Under the regular flood program, up to $250,000 coverage is available for dwellings.

Educational Objective 5

5-1. A FAIR plan (or a beachfront and windstorm plan) makes property insurance coverage available when insurers in the voluntary market cannot profitably provide coverage at a rate that is reasonable for policyholders and provide the needed support for credit.

5-2. FAIR plans were created to respond to three types of losses:
- Riot and civil commotion in urban areas
- Windstorm damage to coastal properties
- Brush fires in some wooded, suburban areas

5-3. Whether the FAIR plan operates as a policy-issuing syndicate or contracts with one or more voluntary insurers to act as servicing organizations for a percentage of premiums, the organizations perform underwriting, policyholder service, and claim handling functions. In most FAIR plans, all licensed property insurers are required to share payment for plan losses in proportion to their share of property insurance premiums collected.

5-4. If a property fails to meet the basic safety levels, the owner can be required to make improvements as a condition for obtaining insurance under the FAIR plan. If the problems are not corrected, the state can deny insurance, provided the exposures are not related to the neighborhood location or to hazardous environmental conditions beyond the owner's control.

5-5. FAIR plans usually cover fire, vandalism, riot, and windstorm.

5-6. Some states offer beachfront and windstorm plans that operate using a single servicing organization that provides the underwriting, policyholders services, and claim handling services. Others operate as policy-issuing syndicates in which the plan issues the policies and the plan's staff provides services. In all plans, insurers that write property coverages in that state are required to share in plan losses in proportion to their share of state property insurance premiums.

5-7. Properties eligible for coverage under beachfront and windstorm plans must be ineligible for coverage in the voluntary market and must be located in designated coastal areas. In some states they must be located within a certain distance of the shoreline. Each plan requires that buildings constructed or rebuilt after a specified date conform to an applicable building code.

5-8. The two primary perils insured against under beachfront and windstorm plans are wind and hail.

5-9. Under beachfront and windstorm plans, when a hurricane has formed within a certain distance of the beach area where the property is located, special provisions might restrict applications for new coverage and/or increases in limits.

5-10. a. Sarah must have the property inspected by the state FAIR plan administrator. The property must meet FAIR plan inspection criteria, which include basic safety levels, or she must make any recommended improvements to the property before it will be eligible.

   b. Because Sarah's state FAIR plan provides coverage against limited perils, Sarah should apply for a difference in conditions policy (DIC) through a specialty insurer. This policy excludes direct loss caused by fire and the other perils covered under the FAIR plan, but it covers the other common homeowners perils.

Direct Your Learning

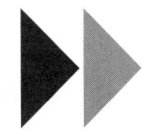

ASSIGNMENT 9

Other Personal Property and Liability Insurance

Educational Objectives

After learning the content of this assignment, you should be able to:

1. Summarize the coverages provided by personal inland marine policies.

2. Compare the coverages typically provided for watercraft under each of the following:
   - HO-3
   - Personal Auto Policy
   - Small boat policies
   - Boatowners and yacht policies

3. Summarize the coverage provided by the typical personal umbrella policy.

4. Given a case describing a liability claim, determine:
   - Whether the loss would be covered by a personal umbrella policy
   - The dollar amount, if any, payable under the umbrella policy
   - The dollar amount, if any, payable under the underlying insurance policies
   - The dollar amount, if any, payable by the insured

Study Materials

Required Reading:
- Personal Insurance
  - Chapter 9

Study Aids:
- SMART Online Practice Exams
- SMART Study Aids
  - Review Notes and Flash Cards—Assignment 9

Outline

- **Inland Marine Floaters**
  - A. Characteristics and Components
  - B. Common Policy Provisions
  - C. Coverages
    1. Personal Articles Standard Loss Settlement Form
    2. Personal Property Form
    3. Personal Effects Form
- **Personal Watercraft Insurance**
  - A. HO-3 Watercraft Coverage
    1. Homeowners Section I—Property Coverages
    2. Homeowners Section II—Liability Coverages
  - B. Personal Auto Policy Watercraft Coverage
  - C. Small Boat Policies
    1. Covered Property
    2. Covered Perils
    3. Exclusions
  - D. Boatowners and Yacht Policies
    1. Warranties
    2. Persons Insured
    3. Physical Damage Coverage
    4. Liability Coverage
    5. Medical Payments Coverage
    6. Other Coverages
- **Personal Umbrella Liability Insurance**
  - A. Purposes of Personal Umbrella Coverage
  - B. Personal Umbrella Coverages
    1. Insuring Agreement
    2. Exclusions
    3. Conditions
- **Umbrella Coverage Case**
  - A. Case Facts
  - B. Case Analysis Tools
  - C. Determination of Coverage
    1. Auto Accident
    2. Slander Lawsuit
  - D. Determination of Amounts Payable
    1. Auto Accident
    2. Slander Lawsuit
- **Summary**

Use the SMART Online Practice Exams to test your understanding of the course material. You can review questions over a single assignment or multiple assignments, or you can take an exam over the entire course. The questions are scored, and you are shown your results. (You score essay exams yourself.)

For each assignment, you should define or describe each of the Key Words and Phrases and answer each of the Review and Application Questions.

Educational Objective 1
Summarize the coverages provided by personal inland marine policies.

Key Words and Phrases

Inland marine insurance

Residence premises

Scheduled coverage

Blanket basis

Inherent vice

Personal effects

Review Questions

1-1. Explain why some insureds might need personal inland marine insurance.

1-2. Identify the general characteristics shared by personal inland marine policies.

1-3. Describe the types of coverage listed in the conditions section of ISO's Common Policy Provisions of a personal inland marine policy.

1-4. How is the amount payable for a covered loss determined, according to the Common Policy Conditions applying to scheduled coverage?

1-5. What are the two types of coverage forms available in the ISO personal inland marine program?

1-6. Describe the type of coverage provided by the Personal Property Form of ISO's personal inland marine program.

1-7. Explain why the Personal Effects Form of ISO's personal inland marine program is designed for frequent travelers.

Application Question

1-8. Larry sold his home and most of his furniture. He is spending at least two years traveling by bicycle across the United States and Europe. He is traveling with camera equipment valued at $8,000. He also placed some furniture, books, and personal possessions in a self-storage unit. What personal inland marine policies can Larry purchase to cover his property?

Educational Objective 2

Compare the coverages typically provided for watercraft under each of the following:

- HO-3
- Personal Auto Policy
- Small boat policies
- Boatowners and yacht policies

Key Words and Phrases

Perils of the sea

Warranties

Hull insurance

Protection and indemnity (P&I) insurance

Uninsured boaters coverage

United States Longshore and Harbor Workers' Compensation Act

Review Questions

2-1. Describe the watercraft physical damage coverage provisions listed in Section I—Property of the HO-3.

2-2. What are the watercraft loss exposures covered in Section II—Liability Coverages of the HO-3?

2-3. Identify the types of watercraft coverage available in a Personal Auto Policy (PAP).

2-4. What are the property and liability loss exposures covered under small boat policies?

2-5. Identify and describe the warranties that apply to personal watercraft insurance.

2-6. Identify the entities insured in the boatowners and yacht policy.

2-7. Briefly summarize each of these coverages typically found in boatowners and yacht insurance policies.

   a. Physical damage coverage (hull insurance)

   b. Liability coverage (P&I insurance)

   c. Medical payments coverage

2-8. Identify the typical exclusions in boatowners and yacht policies that apply to these coverages.

   a. Physical damage coverage (hull insurance)

b. Liability coverage (P&I insurance)

Application Question

2-9. Mary insured her motorboat under a boatowners package policy. Explain whether each of these losses would be covered under Mary's policy. If a loss is not covered, explain why.

a. The front of the boat was badly damaged when the boat collided with a log floating in the water.

b. The propeller on the boat is rusting and must be replaced.

c. A small child riding in Mary's boat fell overboard and drowned. Mary was sued by the deceased child's parents.

Educational Objective 3
Summarize the coverage provided by the typical personal umbrella policy.

Review Questions

3-1. Joe is considering purchasing a personal umbrella policy. Who would be covered under this policy?

3-2. Explain how drop-down coverage applies to a personal umbrella policy.

3-3. Briefly describe the most important conditions in the personal umbrella policy.

Application Question

3-4. Explain whether each of these losses be covered by a typical personal umbrella policy.

   a. The insured detained a youth they falsely accused of stealing a racing bike until the police arrived. The police later arrested the actual thief. The youth's parents sued the insured for the false arrest of their son.

   b. The insured owns a small bakery and is sued when an employee severely burns his hand when an oven's handle falls off.

Educational Objective 4

Given a case describing a liability claim, determine:

- Whether the loss would be covered by a personal umbrella policy
- The dollar amount, if any, payable under the umbrella policy
- The dollar amount, if any, payable under the underlying insurance policies
- The dollar amount, if any, payable by the insured

Application Questions

The student should assume that all the case facts remain the same as those in the umbrella coverage case study unless a question states otherwise. The student also should refer to the policy language provided in the case study's exhibits to answer a question.

4-1. Suppose that Matt and Zoey had failed to pay the premium for their auto policy, and the coverage was canceled. They did make payment on both their HO-3 and umbrella policies to keep them in force. All other details of the case are unchanged. How would amounts payable differ for the auto accident described in this case?

4-2. During the policy period, Matt and Zoey rented a twenty-horsepower motorboat to do some waterskiing. While operating the boat, Matt turned around to check on Zoey and collided with another boat. Three of the other boat's occupants were severely injured, one fatally. Matt and Zoey were found liable for $2 million in bodily injury damages. Determine the amounts payable under Matt and Zoey's homeowners and umbrella policies and any out-of-pocket expenses payable by Matt and Zoey.

Answers to Assignment 9 Questions

NOTE: These answers are provided to give students a basic understanding of acceptable types of responses. They often are not the only valid answers and are not intended to provide an exhaustive response to the questions.

Educational Objective 1

1-1. Some insureds might need personal inland marine insurance because of the restrictive nature of some personal property coverages under a homeowners policy. Personal inland marine policies can provide higher limits of insurance for losses of a particular type or that occur at a particular location.

1-2. Personal inland marine policies share these general characteristics:
- The coverage is tailored to the specific type of property to be insured, such as jewelry, cameras, or musical instruments.
- The insured may select the appropriate policy limits.
- Policies are often written without a deductible.
- Most policies insure property worldwide with special form coverage (open perils), subject to exclusions.

1-3. The Conditions section of the Common Policy Provisions specifies that insured property may have scheduled coverage by which articles or items are specifically listed. The Conditions section also specifies that insured property may have unscheduled coverage by which articles are covered on a blanket basis, such as stamps or coins in a collection.

1-4. With certain exceptions, the amount paid for a covered loss is the least of four amounts:
- The actual cash value of the insured property at the time of loss or damage
- The amount for which the insured could reasonably be expected to have the property repaired to its condition immediately before loss
- The amount for which the insured could reasonably be expected to replace the property with property substantially identical to the lost or damaged article
- The amount of insurance stated in the policy

1-5. In the ISO personal inland marine program, two types of coverage forms are available:
- Specialized forms are used to cover a single category of personal property, such as outboard motors and boats, fine arts, cameras, or motorized golf carts.
- General forms are broader and generic in nature. These three general forms (Personal Articles Standard Loss Settlement Form, Personal Property Form, and Personal Effects Form) are commonly used to provide coverage on a single form for many kinds of personal property.

1-6. The Personal Property Form provides special form coverage on unscheduled personal property owned or used by the insured and normally kept at the insured's residence. The form also provides worldwide coverage on the same property when it is temporarily away from the residence premises. The Personal Property Form can be used to insure thirteen classes of unscheduled personal property, such as silverware, cameras, and major appliances.

1-7. The Personal Effects Form is designed for frequent travelers because it provides special form coverage on personal property such as luggage, clothes, cameras, and sports equipment normally worn or carried by tourists and travelers. The form covers property worldwide, but only while the property is away from the insured's permanent residence.

1-8. A Personal Effects Form can be used to cover the camera. The Personal Property Form can be used to insure the property in the self-storage unit.

Educational Objective 2

2-1. Section I watercraft physical damage coverage includes these provisions:
- A $1,500 limit applies to watercraft, including trailers, furnishings, equipment. (For example, an insured's $800 kayak is fully covered for physical damage loss.)
- Coverage is provided on a named-perils-only basis. (The insured's kayak is covered only for the HO-3 Section I perils, not for perils of the sea.)
- Windstorm coverage applies (up to the $1,500 limit) only when the craft is inside a fully enclosed building.
- Theft coverage does not apply to the boat and motor when away from the residence premises; accessories, trailers, and other boating personal property are excluded from this coverage. (For example, the insured's kayak would not be covered if it is stolen from the roof of the insureds' car while the insureds are traveling.)

2-2. The liability section of the homeowners policy includes a detailed watercraft exclusion focusing on craft of certain size and length. HO-3 Section II watercraft liability coverage, by virtue of the scope of the exclusion, covers only certain limited watercraft loss exposures:
- All watercraft not powered, except sailing vessels twenty-six feet or more in length
- All inboard, inboard-outdrive, and sailing vessels not owned or rented by an insured
- All inboard and inboard-outdrive boats of fifty horsepower or less, rented to an insured
- All sailing vessels with auxiliary power, if less than twenty-six feet long
- All boats powered by an outboard motor or motors, unless the motor both exceeds twenty-five horsepower and was owned by an insured at policy inception

2-3. The Personal Auto Policy provides physical damage loss to a boat trailer if the trailer is described on the PAP Declarations page. Also, a boat trailer the insured owns is covered for liability (regardless of whether it is described on the declarations page) if it is designed to be pulled by a private passenger auto, pickup, or van.

2-4. Typical property loss exposures covered under a small boat policy could include damage to the boat as a result of a collision with another object, theft of the boat's motor or equipment, lightning damage to the boat's electrical and navigational equipment, and wind damage to a sail.

Generally, a small boat policy includes liability insurance for bodily injury, loss of life, illness, and property damage to third parties arising out of the ownership, maintenance, or use of the boat. Medical payments coverage is typically included for any insured person who sustains bodily injury while in, upon, boarding, or leaving the boat. Liability loss exposures covered under a small boat policy can include bodily injury liability for injuries sustained by passengers when a boat collides with a dock, property damage liability for damage to the dock resulting from the collision, and liability for medical payments to a patron on the dock who sustains a minor leg injury as a result of the collision.

2-5. These are the major personal watercraft insurance warranties:
- Pleasure use—The insured warrants that the boat will be used only for private, pleasure purposes and will not be hired or chartered unless the insurer approves.
- Seaworthiness—The insured warrants that the boat is in a seaworthy condition.
- Lay-up period—The insured warrants that the boat will not be in operation during certain periods, such as during the winter months.
- Navigational limits—These warranties limit the use of the vessel to a certain geographical area (for example, inland waterways, and coastal areas only).

2-6. The entities insured in a boatowners and yacht policy include those named on the declarations page, resident relatives of the household, and persons under the age of twenty-one in the insured's care. The insured's paid captain and crew are also considered insureds. Other persons or organizations using the boat without a charge are covered provided the named insured gives permission.

2-7. a. Boatowners and yacht policies contain physical damage coverage (also called hull insurance) on either a named perils or a special form basis covering the boat or "hull," equipment, accessories, motor, and trailer.
   b. Protection and indemnity (P&I) insurance is a broader form of bodily injury and property damage coverage that protects an insured against bodily injury and property damage liability arising from the ownership, maintenance, or use of the boat, and also against crew injuries, wreck removal, and negligence for an unseaworthy vessel. Defense costs arising from any claim, including suits from third parties, are also covered.
   c. Medical payments coverage under boatowners and yacht insurance policies includes coverage for such bodily-injury related expenses as medical, surgical, X-ray, dental, ambulance, hospital, professional nursing, and funeral services; and for first aid rendered at the time of the accident.

2-8. Typical exclusions in boatowners and yacht policies apply to these coverages:
   a. Physical damage coverage (hull insurance)
   - Wear and tear, gradual deterioration, rust, corrosion, mold, wet or dry rot, marring, denting, scratching, inherent vice, latent or physical defect, insects, animal or marine life, weathering, and dampness of atmosphere.
   - Mechanical breakdown or faulty manufacturing, unless the loss was caused by fire or explosion.
   - Freezing and thawing of ice, unless the insured has taken reasonable care to protect the property.
   - Loss that occurs while the boat is used in any official race or speed contest. However, most watercraft policies do not exclude sailboat racing.
   - Intentional loss caused by an insured.
   - War, nuclear hazard, and radioactive contamination.
   b. Liability coverage (P&I insurance)
   - Intentional injury or illegal activities.
   - Renting the watercraft to others or carrying persons or property for a fee without the insurer's permission.

- Liability arising out of water-skiing, parasailing (a sport using a type of parachute to sail through the air while being towed by a powerboat), or other airborne or experimental devices.
- Using watercraft (except sailboats in some policies) in any official race or speed test.
- Losses covered by a workers compensation or similar law.
- Bodily injury or property damage arising out of transportation of the boat on land. (Coverage can be included with the payment of an additional premium.)
- Liability assumed under a contract.
- Injury to an employee if the employee's work involves operation or maintenance of the watercraft (unless otherwise covered by the P&I coverage).
- Business use.
- Discharge or escape of pollutants unless sudden or accidental.
- War, insurrection, rebellion, and nuclear perils.

2-9. a. The hull is covered against damage from a floating log under physical damage coverage.
   b. A rusting propeller is not covered because of the exclusion of general results of direct loss, which excludes loss caused by wear and tear, among others.
   c. The drowning death of a child passenger is covered under liability if Mary is found to be legally liable. Otherwise, the loss is covered under medical payments coverage.

Educational Objective 3

3-1. The policy covers the named insured, resident relatives, and usually persons using (with the insured's permission) cars, motorcycles, recreational vehicles, or watercraft owned by or rented to the named insured. Also, persons younger than twenty-one who are in the care of the named insured or of a resident relative generally are covered.

3-2. The personal umbrella policy typically provides drop-down coverage, which is broader than the underlying coverage. When the underlying insurance does not apply to a particular loss and the loss is not excluded by the umbrella coverage, the umbrella coverage "drops down" to cover the entire loss, less a self-insured retention (SIR). Usually the retention is $250, but it can be as high as $10,000. The SIR applies only when the loss is not covered by an existing underlying policy.

3-3. These are among the most important conditions in the personal umbrella policy:
- The insured must maintain the underlying insurance coverages and limits shown in the declarations. If underlying coverage is not maintained, the policy will pay no more than would have been covered if the underlying insurance was in effect.
- The insured must give the insurer written notice of loss as soon as practicable.
- The umbrella policy is excess over any other insurance, whether collectible or not.
- The policy territory is worldwide.

3-4. a. Yes. The personal umbrella policy would cover the insured's liability for personal injury, including false arrest.
   b. No. The personal umbrella policy would not cover any obligation for which the insured is legally liable under a workers compensation, disability benefits, or similar law.

Educational Objective 4

4-1. The conclusions of the first, second, and fourth DICE steps, as applied in the original case, also apply in this scenario.

The third DICE step is to determine whether all policy conditions have been met. One umbrella policy condition is that the insured must maintain the underlying insurance and policy limits shown in the declarations. Matt and Zoey's umbrella declarations show a PAP policy with a $500,000 limit; Matt and Zoey have failed to meet this umbrella policy condition.

If underlying limits are not maintained, the umbrella policy will pay no more than would have been covered if the underlying insurance was in effect. The canceled PAP pays nothing. Because the loss amount exceeds the umbrella deductible, the personal umbrella liability policy will respond. The $500,000 deductible shown on the umbrella declarations page will be applied, and the umbrella policy will pay $1.3 million for this occurrence. Matt is responsible for the remaining $500,000.

4-2. The first DICE step includes determination of whether the party involved is an insured and whether the accident occurred during the policy period. Both the umbrella policy declarations and the HO-3 declarations show Matt and Zoey as insureds. The accident did occur during the policy period.

The second DICE step is to determine whether the events have triggered coverage under the insuring agreement of one or more of the insurance policies. In the HO-3 Section II Insuring Agreement, the insurer agrees to pay damages for bodily injury and property damage for which an insured is legally responsible because of a covered occurrence. The insuring agreement in the personal umbrella liability policy covers bodily injury and property damage for which an insured becomes legally liable. Therefore the accident appears to trigger coverage under the HO-3 and umbrella policies.

The third DICE step is to determine whether all policy conditions, such as timely reporting of the loss to the insurer, have been met. For the purposes of this question, the student should assume that they have been.

The fourth DICE step is to determine whether one or more exclusions preclude coverage that the insuring agreements have granted. In this case, no exclusions in the HO-3 or umbrella policy would preclude coverage.

The $2 million liability exceeds Matt and Zoey's homeowners liability limit of $500,000 per occurrence. The HO-3 will pay the full policy limits of $500,000 for this event. Because the loss amount exceeds the umbrella deductible, the personal umbrella liability policy will respond. The $500,000 deductible shown on the umbrella declarations page will be applied, and the umbrella policy will pay $1.5 million for this occurrence. Because the HO-3 and the umbrella have covered the full $2 million, nothing is payable by Matt and Zoey.

SEGMENT C

Assignment 10   Personal Loss Exposures and Financial Planning

Assignment 11   Life Insurance

Assignment 12   Health and Disability Insurance

Segment C is the third of three segments in the INS 22 course. These segments are designed to help structure your study.

Direct Your Learning

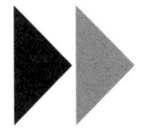

Assignment 10

Personal Loss Exposures and Financial Planning

Educational Objectives

After learning the content of this assignment, you should be able to:

1. Describe each of the following:
    - Loss exposures that are considered personal (human) loss exposures
    - Steps required to develop a financial plan
    - Financial goals that are important to most individuals and families
2. Describe each of the following:
    - Basic types of investment objectives
    - Types of investment risks
    - Types of investments
3. Explain why retirement planning is important.
4. Describe strategies that financial planners suggest regarding investing for retirement.
5. Describe the following types of tax-deferred retirement plans:
    - Private pension plans
    - Individual retirement accounts (IRAs), including traditional IRAs and Roth IRAs
6. Briefly describe other types of tax-deferred retirement plans.
7. Briefly describe various types of individual annuities.
8. In regard to the Social Security program:
    - Describe the basic characteristics of OASDI.
    - Describe the eligibility requirements for insured status.
    - Describe the types of benefits provided.
    - Given a case, explain whether Social Security benefits would be available for a given individual.

Study Materials

Required Reading:
- Personal Insurance
  - Chapter 10

Study Aids:
- SMART Online Practice Exams
- SMART Study Aids
  - Review Notes and Flash Cards—Assignment 10

Outline

- **Personal Loss Exposures**
  - A. Premature Death
  - B. Poor Health and Disability
  - C. Unemployment
    1. Unemployment Compensation
    2. Extended Benefits
  - D. Retirement
- **Planning for the Future**
  - A. Developing a Financial Plan
  - B. Advantages of Financial Planning
  - C. Obstacles to Financial Planning
  - D. Common Financial Goals
- **Investing to Attain Financial Goals**
  - A. Investment Objectives
  - B. Investment Risks
  - C. Types of Investments
  - D. Savings Accounts and Savings Instruments
  - E. Stocks
  - F. Bonds
  - G. Mutual Funds
  - H. Real Estate
  - I. Miscellaneous Investments
- **Retirement Planning**
  - A. Importance of Retirement Planning
    1. Increased Proportion of Retirees
    2. Longer Period of Retirement
    3. Insufficient Money Income
    4. Insufficient Financial Assets
    5. Poor Health
    6. Minimum Floor of Income From Social Security
  - B. Investing for Retirement
- **Tax-Deferred Retirement Plans**
  - A. Private Pension Plans
    1. Eligibility Requirements
    2. Basic Types of Pension Plans
    3. Retirement Age
    4. Vesting
    5. Annual Limits on Contributions and Benefits
    6. Early and Late Distributions
  - B. Traditional Individual Retirement Account
    1. Tax Deductible Contributions
    2. Withdrawing Ira Funds
  - C. Roth IRA
  - D. Other Tax-Deferred Retirement Plans
- **Individual Annuities**
- **Social Security**
  - A. Basic Characteristics of OASDI
    1. Compulsory Program
    2. Minimum Floor of Income
    3. Emphasis on Social Adequacy
    4. Benefits Loosely Related to Earnings
    5. Benefits Prescribed by Law
    6. Financially Self-Supporting
    7. Full Funding Unnecessary
    8. No Means Test
  - B. Covered Occupations
  - C. Insured Status
    1. Fully Insured
    2. Currently Insured
    3. Disability Insured
  - D. Types of Benefits
    1. Retirement Benefits
    2. Survivor Benefits
    3. Disability Income Benefits
    4. Medicare Benefits
- **Summary**

For each assignment, you should define or describe each of the Key Words and Phrases and answer each of the Review and Application Questions.

Educational Objective 1

Describe each of the following:

- Loss exposures that are considered personal (human) loss exposures
- Steps required to develop a financial plan
- Financial goals that are important to most individuals and families

Key Words and Phrases

Personal loss exposure (human loss exposure)

Premature death

Unemployment compensation program

Financial planning

Net worth

Review Questions

1-1. Give four examples of personal (human) loss exposures.

1-2. a. What are the eligibility requirements for unemployment compensation?

b. Distinguish between regular benefits and extended benefits in state unemployment compensation programs.

1-3. What are the steps in the process of financial planning?

1-4. Identify five common financial goals.

Application Question

1-5. Henry and Marie are married and have two children in middle school. Both Henry and Marie work full-time. They own a home and two cars. They have a small saving account and no other investments. They realize they need to develop a financial plan.

   a. What personal (human) loss exposures do the Johnstons face?

   b. Describe the financial planning process that the Johnstons should follow to develop their financial plan.

Educational Objective 2

Describe each of the following:

- Basic types of investment objectives
- Types of investment risks
- Types of investments

Key Words and Phrases

Saving

Investing

Capital appreciation

Preservation of capital

Liquidity

Investment risk

Common stock

Preferred stock

Bond

Mutual fund

Review Questions

2-1. Describe four basic types of investment objectives.

2-2. Identify and describe three types of investment risks.

2-3. Describe these types of investments:

a. Certificates of deposit

b. Common stock

c. Preferred stock

d. Bonds

e. Mutual funds

Application Question

2-4. Randy and Rhonda are starting their own consulting company from their home. They sold a rental house and received $50,000 from that to have a large amount of liquid capital to work with as they grow their company. They would like to place the $50,000 in an investment that retains its liquidity with minimal market and inflation risks. Recommend three types of investments to meet these goals.

Educational Objective 3
Explain why retirement planning is important.

Key Word or Phrase

Tax-deferred retirement plan

Review Questions

3-1. What are some of the trends that might make the goal of a comfortable retirement difficult to attain?

3-2. Explain how early retirement can create potential financial troubles for retirees.

3-3. Identify a medical situation and resulting consequence for which Medicare might not provide elder care.

Application Question

3-4. Bill is a self-employed carpenter who specializes in residential renovations. Because Bill manages his own business and he generally hires others as contractors only when he needs help, he has had no need to establish a retirement plan. In addition, Bill frequently works "under the table," meaning that he collects some payments for his work but does not report the income to avoid taxes and Social Security payments. Evaluate the retirement consequences for Bill as a result of his actions.

Educational Objective 4
Describe strategies that financial planners suggest regarding investing for retirement.

Review Questions

4-1. What are three sound suggestions that financial planners give to investors?

4-2. Why is it important for young workers to take more risk when investing?

4-3. Describe dollar-cost averaging and its advantage to investors.

Application Question

4-4. Joseph completed his college degree in computer science and entered the workforce with a salary over $60,000. In his early twenties, Joseph is more interested in purchasing a sports car than investing for retirement. Prepare an argument to convince Joseph to begin his retirement investment now.

Educational Objective 5
Describe the following types of tax-deferred retirement plans:
- **Private pension plans**
- **Individual retirement accounts (IRAs), including traditional IRAs and Roth IRAs**

Key Words and Phrases

Defined contribution plan (money purchase pension plan)

Defined benefit plan

Vesting

Traditional individual retirement account (IRA)

Roth IRA

Review Questions

5-1. What restrictions apply to withdrawal of funds from a traditional IRA?

5-2. What are the tax advantages of a Roth IRA?

5-3. Under what circumstances are funds withdrawn from a Roth IRA not subject to federal income tax?

Application Question

5-4. The Darlings are a recently married couple in their 30s. They live in an apartment and have two cars. They finished college and are just beginning to advance in their careers. Explain the benefits that the Darlings could expect by starting Roth IRAs now.

Educational Objective 6
Briefly describe other types of tax-deferred retirement plans.

Review Questions

6-1. Briefly describe these tax-deferred retirement plans:

   a. Section 401(k) plan

   b. Profit sharing plan

   c. Thrift (savings) plan

   d. Keogh (HR-10) plan

6-2. Explain why the "SIMPLE" plan is an appropriate name for this retirement vehicle.

6-3. Describe three advantages to an employee of investing in a Section 403(b) plan.

Application Question

6-4. Tool Masters is a metal-working shop that builds custom-designed tools for other manufacturers. The work requires the skills of highly experienced and talented craftsmen. John, the president of Tool Masters, wants to provide tax-deferred retirement plans for his workers as a benefit to remain competitive as an employer. John would like to establish a plan in which each employee can make contributions and Tool Masters can make matching contributions. Describe the tax-deferred retirement plans that meet these requirements.

Educational Objective 7
Briefly describe various types of individual annuities.

Key Word or Phrase
Annuity

Review Questions

7-1. What is the purpose of an annuity?

7-2. Explain how cash invested in a deferred annuity can be distributed at retirement.

7-3. Explain why a variable annuity could be a better investment than a fixed annuity.

Application Question

7-4. Jeff, who is forty-five years old, received a $200,000 inheritance from his grandmother. Up until this time, Jeff has not had a retirement plan, and he would like to use this inheritance to establish such a plan. Explain how Jeff can use an annuity for such a purpose.

Educational Objective 8

In regard to the Social Security program:

- Describe the basic characteristics of OASDI.
- Describe the eligibility requirements for insured status.
- Describe the types of benefits provided.
- Given a case, explain whether Social Security benefits would be available for a given individual.

Review Questions

8-1. Explain the advantages of a compulsory Social Security program in the United States.

8-2. Briefly explain the principle of social adequacy that is followed in the Social Security program.

8-3. Explain these types of insured status under the Social Security program:

   a. Fully insured

   b. Currently insured

   c. Disability insured

8-4. Briefly explain each of these factors that affect the amount of retirement benefits under the Social Security program.

   a. Normal (full) retirement age

   b. Primary insurance amount

c. Average indexed monthly earnings

d. Cost-of-living adjustment

e. Early retirement age

f. Delayed retirement credit

8-5. Briefly describe the survivor benefits that may be paid under the Social Security program.

Application Questions

8-6. Martha and John both reached full-retirement age this year. They are not currently receiving any Social Security benefits. John is fully and currently insured for Social Security purposes.

   a. What will determine the amount of the Social Security retirement benefits that they can receive?

   b. How will their benefits be affected if John delays his retirement and continues to work after full-retirement age? Explain.

8-7. Oscar, age thirty-three, and his wife, age thirty, have two children, ages four and two. Oscar is fully and currently insured for purposes of the Social Security program.

   a. Explain what is meant by Oscar's being fully and currently insured for purposes of the Social Security program.

   b. Briefly describe the types of survivor benefits available to the members of Oscar's family under the Social Security program if Oscar should die today.

Answers to Assignment 10 Questions

NOTE: These answers are provided to give students a basic understanding of acceptable types of responses. They often are not the only valid answers and are not intended to provide an exhaustive response to the questions.

Educational Objective 1

1-1. Four examples of personal loss exposures include:
- Premature death—A worker dies at age forty-two following a medical emergency.
- Sickness or injury—A worker sustains serious injuries from an auto accident.
- Unemployment—A worker is laid off from a factory and has no other source of income.
- Retirement—A worker retires voluntarily and has insufficient income to pay ongoing expenses.

1-2. a. The eligibility requirements for unemployment compensation include:
- Become involuntarily unemployed
- Earn qualifying wages during a specified base period
- Actively seek work
- Be free from disqualifying acts (such as refusing suitable work)
- Meet a specified waiting period (generally one week)

b. State unemployment compensation programs pay regular weekly cash benefits to covered workers who are involuntarily unemployed. A federal-state unemployment compensation program pays additional extended benefits (up to thirteen weeks) to claimants who have exhausted their regular benefits during periods of high unemployment.

1-3. The steps in the financial planning process include:
- Gather important financial information (current income, assets, outstanding liabilities and debts, current spending, and number and ages of dependents).
- Analyze the present financial situation.
- Determine specific financial goals and objectives.
- Design a financial plan for attaining these goals.
- Periodically review and revise the plan.

1-4. Five common financial goals could include:
- Increasing personal wealth
- Saving for retirement
- Funding college education for children
- Getting out of debt
- Minimizing taxes

1-5. a. The Johnstons could face lost income from these loss exposures:
- Premature death—Henry could die suddenly from a heart attack.
- Poor health or disability—Marie could have an auto accident, sustain serious injuries, and be unable to continue working.
- Unemployment—Henry could involuntarily lose his job from a company cutback.
- Retirement—The Johnstons could retire voluntarily and learn they have insufficient income to pay expenses.

b. Henry and Marie should follow this financial planning process to develop their financial plan:
- Gather important financial information:
  - Current income
  - Assets
  - Outstanding liabilities and debts
  - Current spending
  - Number and ages of dependents
- Analyze the present financial situation.
- Determine specific financial goals and objectives.
- Design a financial plan for attaining these goals.
- Periodically review and revise the plan.

Educational Objective 2

2-1. Four basic types of investment objectives could include these:
- Capital appreciation—An increase in the value of investments
- Preservation of capital—Making sure that the value of assets does not decrease
- Growth and income—A high total return from investing primarily in stocks that pay high current dividends and also have the potential for capital appreciation
- Liquidity—The ability to quickly convert an investment into cash with a minimal loss of principal

2-2. Three types of investment risks could include these:
- Inflation risk—The loss of purchasing power because of an overall price-level increase in the economy
- Interest rate risk—A change in the future value of a security because of changes in interest rates
- Financial risk—Risk associated with the ownership of securities in a company with a relatively large amount of debt on its balance sheet. (If the company defaults on its debt obligations, it may be forced into bankruptcy by its creditors.)

2-3. Financial investments could involve any of these:
   a. Certificates of deposit—Time deposits that mature after a certain period, pay higher returns than regular savings accounts, are insured by the FDIC, and may have a penalty for early withdrawal
   b. Common stock—An ownership interest in a corporation giving stockowners certain rights and privileges, such as the right to vote on important corporate matters
   c. Preferred stock—An ownership interest in a corporation providing an annual dividend to the stockowners (paid before dividends are paid to common stockholders) but restricting voting rights
   d. Bonds—Debt obligations issued by corporations and government entities (usually sold in $1,000 denominations)
   e. Mutual funds—An investment organization pooling the funds of individual investors and investing in diversified securities

2-4. Randy and Rhonda would probably best achieve their goals by using investments in the savings instruments category:
   - Regular saving accounts are insured and liquid.
   - Money market mutual funds are readily accessible but typically not insured.
   - Money market deposit accounts are insured and readily accessible.

Educational Objective 3

3-1. The following trends might make the goal of a comfortable retirement difficult to attain:
   - Longer period of retirement
   - Insufficient money income
   - Insufficient financial assets
   - Cost of long-term care

3-2. Early retirees, because of their shorter period of employment, might be unable to save enough during their working years to provide for a decent standard of living during the longer retirement period.

3-3. A medical situation for which Medicare might not provide assistance is with long-term care in a nursing facility. Most retired persons do not have private long-term care policies because of the high cost. As a result, older patients are forced to apply for coverage under the Medicaid program, which is a welfare program with strict eligibility requirements.

3-4. Social Security is the only retirement benefit that Bill will receive. Social Security is intended to provide only a minimum floor of income. By working "under the table" Bill is further reducing his reported earnings and the monthly income he will receive from Social Security. Without any other investments for retirement, Bill might have insufficient money to support himself.

Educational Objective 4

4-1. Financial planners might give investors these sound suggestions:
- Begin investing early.
- Make maximum contributions to tax-deferred retirement plans.
- Change the allocation of assets over the life cycle.
- Consider dollar-cost averaging.
- Do not ignore the impact of inflation after retirement.

4-2. Young workers should take more risk when investing (using vehicles such as common stocks or mutual funds) because of the longer period to retirement. Market fluctuation will allow the young investor to recoup potential drops in stocks.

4-3. Dollar-cost averaging is an investment strategy in which a fixed amount is invested at regular intervals, regardless of market price and market conditions. Investors who use dollar-cost averaging can be at an advantage over other investors because the average cost per share will be less than the average market price.

4-4. Investing early allows accumulated deposits and investment earning that can be compounded over a longer period of time. The differences in savings at retirement can be significantly greater by starting only a few years sooner. In addition, many retirement plans are tax-deferred, which means that your contributions to your retirement plan are made free of income taxes. The contributions and their accumulated interest are taxed only when you withdraw the money at retirement. At that time your income will probably be lower, and your income tax rate should also be lower.

Educational Objective 5

5-1. A 10 percent tax penalty in addition to the ordinary income tax would apply on the taxable amount of traditional IRA funds withdrawn before age fifty-nine and one-half. A different tax penalty applies if the account owner does not make annual minimum withdrawals after reaching age seventy and one-half.

5-2. A Roth IRA has these tax advantages:
- Investment earnings accumulate free of federal income taxes.
- Qualified distributions from Roth IRAs held for at least five years are not taxable for an account holder age fifty-nine and one-half or older.
- The account holder does not need to make minimum annual withdrawals after reaching age seventy and one-half.

5-3. Funds can be withdrawn from Roth IRAs and not be subject to federal income tax if the account has been held for at least five years and the distribution is made for any of these reasons:
- The account holder is age fifty-nine and one-half or older.
- The account holder is disabled.
- The distribution is paid to a beneficiary upon the account holder's death.
- The money is used for a first-time home purchase (maximum $10,000).

5-4. Each of the Darlings can make an annual contribution to a Roth IRA. Earnings on the contributions accumulate tax-free until retirement. At retirement, amounts held five or more years can be withdrawn tax-free by the account holder or, at death, can be paid tax-free to a beneficiary.

Educational Objective 6

6-1. Descriptions of tax-deferred retirement plans include:
   a. Section 401(k) plan—Allows participants the option of contributing before-tax dollars into the plan; thus they receive favorable tax treatment (typically includes employer contributions).
   b. Profit sharing plan—Pays part of the firm's profits to participating employees (defined contribution plan).
   c. Thrift (savings) plan—Allows eligible employees to contribute voluntarily up to a certain percentage of their salary, and the employer contributes some fraction of the employee's contribution (defined contribution plan).
   d. Keogh (HR-10) plan—Allows self-employed individuals to make tax-deductible contributions to a defined contribution plan or a defined benefit plan.

6-2. The "SIMPLE" plan is an appropriate name for this retirement vehicle because the employers who use it are exempt from complex reporting requirements and administrative rules that apply to qualified pension plans.

6-3. Three advantages of investing in Section 403(b) plans are:
- The employer contributes to the plan.
- The employee's taxable income is reduced.
- The plan contributions and investment income accumulate free of income taxes until the employee actually receives the funds.

6-4.
- Section 401(k) plan—Allows participants the option of contributing before-tax dollars and employers the option of making contributions.
- Thrift plan—Employees voluntarily contribute to the plan and the employer contributes a fraction of that amount.

Educational Objective 7

7-1. The fundamental purpose of an annuity is to provide periodic income that an individual cannot outlive (lifetime income) and protection against exhaustion of savings.

7-2. At retirement, cash invested in a deferred annuity can be paid to the annuitant in a lump sum or as income under one of the annuity options stated in the policy.

7-3. A variable annuity could be a better investment over a fixed annuity because variable annuity payments vary depending on the investment returns of the fund in which the premiums are invested. The purpose is to provide protection against inflation by maintaining the real purchasing power of the benefits during retirement. With fixed annuities, the periodic payments are fixed in amount, leaving the annuitant no protection against inflation.

7-4. Jeff can purchase a deferred annuity. The premiums paid less expenses are accumulated tax-free before retirement. At retirement, the cash in the annuity can be paid to the annuitant in a lump sum or as income under one of the annuity options stated in the policy.

Educational Objective 8

8-1. A compulsory Social Security program has these advantages:
- Achieves a base of financial security for the population (social objective)
- Controls adverse selection by covering all healthy and unhealthy people

8-2. The Social Security program pays benefits based on a certain standard of living for all beneficiaries. These benefits provide social adequacy—a minimum floor of income for all covered groups in the population.

8-3. The Social Security program includes these types of insured status:
   a. Fully insured—A worker must have forty credits or have worked full-time for ten years to be fully insured for life.
   b. Currently insured—A worker has earned at least six credits during the last thirteen calendar quarters ending with the quarter in which qualified benefits occur.
   c. Disability insured—A worker age thirty-one or older must be fully insured and have at least twenty credits out of the last forty quarters, ending with the quarter in which the worker became disabled. (Special rules apply to younger workers and to blind people.)

8-4. These factors affect the amount of retirement benefits under the Social Security program:
   a. Normal (full) retirement age—The retirement age at which the worker will receive full retirement benefits. The full retirement age will gradually increase to age sixty-seven in the year 2027.
   b. Primary insurance amount—The monthly retirement benefit amount is based on the worker's average indexed monthly earnings and is paid to the worker at the full retirement age or paid to a disabled worker at any age.
   c. Average indexed monthly earnings—The worker's actual earnings are indexed or updated to consider changes in average wages from the year the earnings were received. (This ensures that workers who retire today will have retirement benefits providing about the same proportion of their earnings as workers who retire in the future.)
   d. Cost-of-living adjustment—An adjustment to automatically increase monthly cash benefits each year for changes in the cost of living, maintaining the real purchasing power of the benefits.
   e. Early retirement age—A worker can retire at age sixty-two and before the normal (full) retirement age with a reduced benefit. (The annual retirement benefit was reduced by 20 percent of the full benefit up to the year 2002, but will gradually be reduced up to 30 percent.)
   f. Delayed retirement credit—A credit for a worker who delays retirement and works beyond the full retirement age up to age seventy. (This credit will gradually be increased.)

8-5. The Social Security program can pay survivor benefits to these beneficiaries:
- Unmarried children under age eighteen
- Unmarried disabled children
- Surviving spouse caring for children under age sixteen or unmarried disabled children
- Surviving spouse age sixty or older if the deceased is fully insured
- Disabled widow or widower, age fifty through fifty-nine
- Dependent parent age sixty-two and older if the deceased is fully insured

In addition to the survivor benefits, a lump sum benefit of $255 can be paid to an eligible surviving spouse or to a child entitled to benefits.

8-6. a. The amount of the Smiths' retirement benefits will be determined by benefit formulas determined by federal law. John's primary insurance amount (PIA) will be determined on the basis of his average indexed monthly earnings.

b. John's PIA will be increased for each year of delayed retirement beyond full-retirement age up to age seventy.

8-7. a. Fully insured status requires that a worker have forty credits (quarters of coverage) or have worked full time for ten years. Currently insured status requires that a worker have at least six quarters of coverage out of the thirteen quarters preceding a Social Security claim.

b. Because Oscar is fully and currently insured, his family would be entitled to the following benefits upon his death:
- Survivor benefits for the children until they reach age eighteen
- Survivor benefits for his wife until the youngest child reaches age sixteen
- Survivor benefits for his wife at age sixty or older
- A lump-sum death benefit

Direct Your Learning

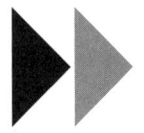

ASSIGNMENT 11

Life Insurance

Educational Objectives

After learning the content of this assignment, you should be able to:

1. Describe the costs associated with premature death.
2. Describe the need for life insurance with regard to various types of family structures.
3. Describe the needs approach for determining the amount of life insurance to own.
4. Describe the following types of life insurance:
   - Term insurance
   - Whole life insurance, including ordinary life and limited-payment life insurance
   - Universal life insurance
5. Describe life insurance contractual provisions.
6. Explain the purpose of additional benefits that can be added to a life insurance policy by appropriate riders.
7. Describe factors used in underwriting individual life insurance.
8. Describe the following aspects of group life insurance:
   - Basic characteristics
   - Underwriting factors
   - Typical eligibility requirements
   - Typical benefits provided
9. Given a case involving a life insurance claim:
   - Explain whether the claim would be paid to the beneficiary.
   - Determine the amount the insurer would pay for covered losses.
   - Explain how a given settlement option would affect payment.

Study Materials

Required Reading:
- Personal Insurance
  - Chapter 11

Study Aids:
- SMART Online Practice Exams
- SMART Study Aids
  - Review Notes and Flash Cards—Assignment 11

Outline

- **Premature Death**
- **Need for Life Insurance**
  - A. Singles
  - B. Single-Parent Families
  - C. Two-Income Families
  - D. Traditional Families
  - E. Blended Families
  - F. Sandwiched Families
- **Determining the Amount of Life Insurance to Own**
  - A. Needs Approach
  - B. Illustration of Needs Approach
- **Types of Life Insurance**
  - A. Term Insurance
    1. Basic Characteristics of Term Insurance
    2. Types of Term Insurance
    3. Uses of Term Insurance
  - B. Whole Life Insurance
    1. Ordinary Life Insurance
    2. Limited-Payment Life Insurance
  - C. Universal Life Insurance
    1. Basic Characteristics of Universal Life Insurance
    2. Uses of Universal Life Insurance
  - D. Other Types of Life Insurance
- **Life Insurance Contractual Provisions**
  - A. Incontestable Clause
  - B. Suicide Clause
  - C. Grace Period
  - D. Reinstatement Clause
  - E. Misstatement of Age or Sex
  - F. Beneficiary Designations
  - G. Assignment Clause
  - H. Dividend Options
  - I. Nonforfeiture Options
  - J. Policy Loan Provision
  - K. Settlement Options
- **Additional Life Insurance Benefits**
  - A. Waiver of Premium
  - B. Accidental Death Benefit
  - C. Guaranteed Insurability
  - D. Cost-of-Living Rider
  - E. Accelerated Death Benefits
- **Life Insurance Underwriting**
  - A. Underwriting Factors
  - B. Underwriting Decisions
- **Group Life Insurance**
  - A. Basic Characteristics
  - B. Group Underwriting Factors
  - C. Eligibility Requirements
  - D. Group Life Insurance Benefits
- **Summary**

The SMART Online Practice Exams product contains a final practice exam. You should take this exam only when you have completed your study of the entire course. Take this exam under simulated exam conditions. It will be your best indicator of how well-prepared you are.

For each assignment, you should define or describe each of the Key Words and Phrases and answer each of the Review and Application Questions.

Educational Objective 1
Describe the costs associated with premature death.

Review Questions

1-1. Life insurance is designed to help reduce the financial consequences of premature death. In this context, when is death considered to be premature?

1-2. Briefly describe the possible costs of premature death.

1-3. Is the financial effect of premature death uniform for all families? Explain.

Application Question

1-4. Stewart and Meg have two daughters under the age of four. Both Stewart and Meg work full time, and they own a small house with a mortgage. They are calculating the funds needed to support their daughters if one or both of the parents should die before the girls are grown. What are the costs that Stewart and Meg should include this calculation?

Educational Objective 2
Describe the need for life insurance with regard to various types of family structures.

Review Questions

2-1. Identify the six types of family structures.

2-2. Explain why the need for life insurance of the spouse staying at home in a traditional family structure can be equally important as that of the spouse employed in the labor force.

2-3. For each of the family structures identified in your answer to Question 2-1, explain the need for life insurance for each.

Application Question

2-4. Explain why an individual might consider purchasing term life insurance despite the fact that it provides temporary coverage.

Educational Objective 3
Describe the needs approach for determining the amount of life insurance to own.

Key Word or Phrase

Needs approach

Review Questions

3-1. Identify the six most important family needs when determining the amount of life insurance to own.

3-2. Why should a family consider the readjustment period as one of its needs when determining the amount of life insurance needed?

3-3. Aside from the readjustment period, describe three needs a family is likely to consider when using the needs approach.

Application Question

3-4. Determine your need for life insurance using the needs approach.

Life Insurance 11.7

Educational Objective 4
Describe the following types of life insurance:
- Term insurance
- Whole life insurance, including ordinary life and limited-payment life insurance
- Universal life insurance

Key Words and Phrases

Term insurance

Cash value

Renewable

Convertible

Mortality rates

Evidence of insurability

Whole life insurance

Ordinary life insurance

Paid-up policy

Limited-payment life insurance

Universal life insurance

Review Questions

4-1. Describe the basic characteristics of term insurance.

4-2. Identify and briefly describe three types of term insurance.

4-3. Identify and describe the two basic types of whole life insurance.

4-4. a. Describe the basic characteristics of universal life insurance.

   b. State two appropriate uses of universal life insurance.

Application Question

4-5. Kirby, age twenty-six, is married and has twin sons, age four. Kirby is the family's principal wage earner. Kirby wants his sons to attend college someday. His net worth is limited.

   a. Explain why term life insurance might be appropriate for Kirby.

   b. Explain why universal life insurance might be appropriate for Kirby.

c. If Kirby buys a whole life policy, explain why he should consider buying (1) the waiver of premium option and (2) the guaranteed insurability rider.

Educational Objective 5
Describe life insurance contractual provisions.

Key Words and Phrases

Incontestable clause

Suicide clause

Grace period

Reinstatement clause

Misstatement of age or sex provision

Beneficiary

Participating policy

Nonparticipating (guaranteed cost) policy

Nonforfeiture options

Settlement options

Review Questions

5-1. Identify and briefly describe four life insurance policy dividend options.

5-2. Identify and briefly describe three life insurance policy nonforfeiture options.

5-3. Identify and briefly describe three life insurance policy settlement options.

Application Question

5-4. Mike has been insured by an ordinary life insurance policy for twenty-five years. Mike stopped paying the premiums for his policy one year ago.

    a. Briefly explain how the reinstatement clause in Mike's life insurance policy would apply in this situation.

    b. If Mike decides to let his life insurance policy lapse, what nonforfeiture options would be available to him?

Educational Objective 6
Explain the purpose of additional benefits that can be added to a life insurance policy by appropriate riders.

Key Words and Phrases
Rider

Waiver of premium

Accidental death benefit

Guaranteed insurability rider (guaranteed purchase option)

Review Questions

6-1. What are the three requirements of the waiver of premium provision?

6-2. Describe the three requirements that must be satisfied to collect accidental death benefits.

6-3. Describe the three basic types of accelerated death benefits riders.

Application Question

6-4. Ruth's family has a history of debilitating heart disease. Although Ruth is in good health, she fears that she might have the same problem as she grows older. What riders would you recommend that Ruth attach to her life insurance policy to protect her in the event that her health does deteriorate?

Educational Objective 7
Describe factors used in underwriting individual life insurance.

Review Questions

7-1. Identify five factors considered in underwriting individual life insurance.

7-2. What are the conditions under which standard life insurance rates can be offered to alcoholics?

7-3. Describe the three possible underwriting decisions that can be made after evaluating the information provided by a life insurance applicant.

Application Question

7-4. Jennifer and Joyce are twins. They both purchased life insurance from the same insurance company for the same limits. However Joyce's was placed in a substandard category and her premiums were higher than Jennifer's premiums. Describe the underwriting factors that might account for Joyce's placement in a substandard category.

Educational Objective 8
Describe the following aspects of group life insurance:
- **Basic characteristics**
- **Underwriting factors**
- **Typical eligibility requirements**
- **Typical benefits provided**

Key Words and Phrases

Noncontributory plan

Contributory plan

Review Questions

8-1. Describe the basic characteristics of group life insurance.

8-2. Describe the factors considered in underwriting group life insurance.

8-3. Identify the eligibility requirements for group life insurance.

Application Question

8-4. Peggy now has $50,000 of group term life insurance through her employer under a noncontributory plan.

   a. What part of the group term life insurance premium, if any, is Peggy required to pay? Explain.

   b. Would Peggy be able to personally continue coverage, now provided under her group policy, if she were to quit her job? Explain.

Educational Objective 9

Given a case involving a life insurance claim:

- Explain whether the claim would be paid to the beneficiary
- Determine the amount an insurer would pay for covered losses
- Explain how a given settlement option would affect payment

Review Questions

9-1. Catherine is a young mother on a limited income. She wants to plan for the future and put her son through college. Would purchasing a term life insurance policy help her accomplish this goal? Explain.

9-2. Would term insurance or ordinary life insurance be better for a single parent with a modest income if the parent wanted to provide financial protection for his son if he should die?

9-3. John is a heavy smoker but conceals this fact on his life insurance application. He dies of lung cancer one year after the policy becomes effective. Is John's insurer required to pay death benefits? Explain.

Application Question

9-4. Reba is married and has a teen-aged son. She had a whole life insurance policy with a ten-year fixed-period and a face value of $300,000 and a cash value of $70,000. She has an accidental death benefit rider and a catastrophic illness rider attached to the policy. Reba contracted cancer, which ended her life within twelve months. Describe the benefits that would be payable from her life insurance policy.

Answers to Assignment 11 Questions

NOTE: These answers are provided to give students a basic understanding of acceptable types of responses. They often are not the only valid answers and are not intended to provide an exhaustive response to the questions.

Educational Objective 1

1-1. Life insurance can reduce the financial consequences of premature death. Premature death is the early death of a person with outstanding or unfulfilled financial obligations, such as dependents to support, children to educate, or a mortgage and other installment debts to pay.

1-2. The possible costs of premature death include these:
- Termination of income—Family's loss of income
- Additional costs—Funeral expenses, uninsured medical bills, probate and estate settlement costs, childcare expenses for young dependent children, and federal and state taxes for large estates
- Potential reduction in the family's standard of living—Insufficient replacement income
- Certain emotional and noneconomic costs—Grief of a surviving spouse, loss of a role model, and loss of moral guidance for the children

1-3. The financial effect of premature death is not uniform for all families; it varies enormously depending on the type of family structure.

1-4. Stewart and Meg should consider these costs:
- The income earned that will be lost
- Funeral expenses, uninsured medical bills, probate and estate settlement costs, child-care expenses

Educational Objective 2

2-1. The six types of family structures are:
- Singles
- Single-parent families
- Two-income families
- Traditional families
- Blended families
- Sandwiched families

2-2. In a traditional family structure, the need for life insurance of the spouse staying at home can be equally important as that of the spouse employed in the labor force because the death of the stay-at-home spouse can result in significant expenses for childcare and housekeeping.

2-3. Different family structures have different needs for life insurance:

(1) Singles—Modest amounts of life insurance needed
- Might have no dependents and no outstanding financial obligations
- Might need funds to cover funeral expenses and uninsured medical bills

(2) Single-parent families—Great need for life insurance
- Might have children under age eighteen (childcare and education costs)
- Need funds to replace the income earned, funeral expenses, and uninsured medical bills

(3) Two-income families—Substantial need for life insurance on both spouses
- Need to maintain the family's customary standard of living
- Indebtedness and current or future financial support of parents or other relatives

(4) Traditional families—Substantial need for life insurance on both spouses
- Might have children under age eighteen (childcare and education costs)
- Need funds to cover funeral expenses, uninsured medical bills, and financial obligations
- Need funds to replace the income of the working parent(s) and maintain the family's standard of living

(5) Blended families—Great need for life insurance
- Need to maintain the family's customary standard of living
- Might have additional children born into the new marriage, resulting in childcare costs and funds for the college education

(6) Sandwiched families—Great need for life insurance
- Need funds to replace the income of the working son or daughter who might provide financial support to his or her parent(s)

2-4. Although term insurance provides only temporary coverage, a person might still consider purchasing term life insurance because:
- The potential policyholder might need to purchase a substantial amount of life insurance with limited income.
- He or she might need temporary protection for a readjustment, dependence, or blackout period.
- The potential policyholder might want to convert the term insurance later to a permanent policy without proving evidence of insurability.

Educational Objective 3

3-1. These are six of the most important family needs when determining the amount of life insurance to own:
- An estate clearance fund
- Income during the readjustment period
- Income during the dependency period
- Income to the surviving spouse during the blackout period
- Retirement income
- Special needs, such as paying off a mortgage, an emergency fund, or a college fund for children

3-2. A family should consider the readjustment period as one of its needs when determining the amount of life insurance needed to help it maintain its customary standard of living and to otherwise adapt to additional changes.

3-3. A family might consider these needs when using the needs approach to estimate the proper amount of life insurance to own:
- Estate clearance fund—Cash for funeral expenses, uninsured medical bills, car loans, installment debts, and estate administration expenses
- Dependency period—Continuing payments to replace lost income until dependent children reach age eighteen
- Blackout period—Additional payments to the surviving spouse for the period when he or she is ineligible for Social Security benefits (after the youngest child reaches age sixteen and before the spouse reaches age sixty)

3-4. Your answer will depend on your individual situation. Completing this exercise can help you understand the concepts addressed in this assignment.

Educational Objective 4

4-1. Term insurance has these basic characteristics:
- Temporary protection—Protection for a specified period (e.g., ten years) or until the insured reaches a specified age (e.g., sixty-five)
- No cash value or savings element—No accumulation of funds
- Renewable and convertible—Can be renewed for additional periods or exchanged for permanent life insurance without evidence of insurability
- Increasing premiums—Based on mortality rates that increase with the insured's age

4-2. Three types of term insurance include:
- Yearly renewable term—The policyowner has the right to renew for successive one-year periods.
- Specified period term—The premium does not change during the policy term unless the policy is renewed at the end of the term.
- Decreasing term—The premium gradually declines during the term of the policy.

4-3. Two types of whole life insurance include:
- Ordinary life insurance—The premiums are paid periodically until the insured dies or reaches age 100.
- Limited-payment life insurance—The premiums are level for a certain number of years, after which the policy is paid-up.

4-4. a. Basic characteristics of universal life insurance include these:
- Separation of protection, savings, and expense components—The policyowner receives an annual disclosure statement that shows the premiums paid, death benefit, expense charges, interest credited to the cash value account, and cash surrender value.
- Stated rate of interest—The policy specifically states the interest rate credited to the cash value account.
- Considerable flexibility—The policyowner can decrease, increase, or skip premiums as long as the cash value account is sufficient to pay the mortality costs and expenses; can increase the death benefit with evidence of insurability; can add to the cash value at any time subject to insurer restrictions; can receive policy loans; and can add certain insureds to the policy.

- Partial cash withdrawals option—A partial cash withdrawal reduces the cash value account but does not obligate the policyowner to pay interest on the funds withdrawn or to repay the insurance company.

  b. Universal life insurance can be used by policyholders for these purposes:
  - For a flexible life insurance program
  - To meet specific financial goals

4-5. a. Term insurance might be the only affordable way to give Kirby the amount of death benefit he needs because premiums would be low at Kirby's current age. Term insurance usually has a convertible feature that would let Kirby convert to some form of permanent insurance without evidence of insurability sometime in the future.

  b. Universal life insurance premiums are higher than term insurance premiums at Kirby's age. However, universal life premiums are flexible, and it may be possible to keep the premium low in the early years to maintain the coverage he needs. Because universal life develops cash values over time, Kirby could withdraw or borrow cash value from his policy to pay the premium due when the sons are in college, freeing up Kirby's income to pay college expenses.

  c. (1) A waiver of premium rider would guarantee that the policy would remain in force with the cash value still growing if Kirby were disabled and unable to earn a living.

  (2) A guaranteed insurability rider would guarantee that Kirby could buy additional death benefit, without giving evidence of insurability, at specified times in the future. This option could be valuable, for example, if Kirby suffered a health impairment in the future and became uninsurable for additional coverage.

Educational Objective 5

5-1. Life insurance policies include four dividend options:
- Cash—The dividend is paid to the policyowner by the insurer (usually on the anniversary date of the policy).
- Reduction of premium—The dividend is used to reduce the next year's premium.
- Accumulate at interest—The dividend accumulates at interest with the insurer at a specified rate stated in the policy (or higher) and can be withdrawn at any time.
- Paid-up additions—The dividend is used to purchase additional amounts of paid-up whole life insurance that become part of the basic death benefit.

5-2. Life insurance policy nonforfeiture options include:
- Cash—The policy can be surrendered for its cash surrender value; protection under the policy terminates.
- Reduced paid-up insurance—The cash value in the policy can be applied as a net single premium to purchase a reduced amount of paid-up insurance.
- Extended term insurance—The cash value is used to extend the face amount of insurance as paid-up term insurance.

5-3. Life insurance policies offer these settlement options:
- Interest option—The insurer retains the death proceeds and interest is paid periodically to the beneficiary as stated in the policy.
- Fixed-period option—The insurer pays the policy proceeds to a designated beneficiary or beneficiaries over some fixed period.
- Fixed-amount option—The insurer pays a fixed amount periodically to the beneficiary.

5-4. a. The reinstatement clause in his life insurance policy would give Mike the right to reinstate the lapsed policy if he had not yet surrendered it for the cash value. To reinstate the policy, Mike would need to pay all unpaid premiums plus interest, repay or reinstate all policy loans, provide evidence of insurability, and do this all within five years of the date the policy lapsed.

b. If he decides to let his life insurance policy lapse, Mike would have these nonforfeiture options:
- Surrender the policy for its cash surrender value. Protection under the policy would cease immediately.
- Have the cash value in the policy applied as a net single premium to purchase a reduced amount of paid-up insurance.
- Have the cash value used to extend the face amount of insurance as paid-up term insurance.

Educational Objective 6

6-1. The three requirements of the waiver of premium provision are:
- Insured must be totally disabled before a certain age.
- Insured must be totally disabled for six months (four months in some policies).
- Definition of disability must be satisfied.

6-2. The three requirements that must be satisfied to collect accidental death benefits are:
- The death must result directly from an accidental bodily injury. Death from disease, suicide, war, inhalation of gas or fumes, commission of a felony, and certain aviation activities other than as a fare-paying passenger are typically excluded.
- The death must occur within a certain number of days, usually ninety, after the accident. Some riders have a longer period, such as 180 days, one year, or as long as the rider is in effect.
- The death must occur before some stated age, such as age sixty-five or seventy.

6-3. The three basic types of accelerated death benefits riders are:
- Terminal illness rider—This rider allows insureds with a life expectancy of six months or one year to collect part or all of the available proceeds.
- Catastrophic illness rider—Insureds who have certain catastrophic diseases, such as life-threatening cancer, coronary artery disease, or AIDS, can receive part of the face amount of insurance.
- Long-term care rider—Insureds who require long-term care can receive part of the face amount to help pay for the cost of care.

6-4. These riders should be recommended:
- The waiver of premium rider will eliminate premium payments if Ruth becomes disabled.
- The guaranteed insurability rider will guarantee Ruth's insurability even if her health deteriorates.
- The terminal illness rider will allow Ruth to receive the benefits if her life expectancy is severely shortened
- The long-term care rider will allow Ruth to receive part of the face amount of the policy to pay for the cost of her care, if she requires it.

Educational Objective 7

7-1. Five underwriting considerations for individual life insurance include these factors:
- Age
- Personal health history
- Hazardous sports and hobbies
- Residence
- Occupation

7-2. Standard life insurance rates can be offered to alcoholics who have successfully undergone treatment or have not consumed alcohol for a number of years.

7-3. The three possible underwriting decisions that can be made after evaluating the information provided by a life insurance applicant are:
- The applicant might be rated as standard and charged the normal premium for the desired coverage.
- The applicant might be rated as substandard and charged a higher premium.
- The applicant might be rejected.

7-4. Underwriting factors that might account for Joyce's substandard category placement could include:
- Build—Joyce might be substantially overweight and therefore in a higher mortality category.
- Physical condition and health history—Joyce's physical condition and health might not be as good as Jennifer's.
- Smoking—Joyce may be a smoker.
- Hazardous sports and hobbies—Joyce may engage in high risk sports.
- Habits and morals—Joyce may have an addiction or stress factors.
- Residence—Joyce may live in a part of the world where she is more prone to contract a disease.
- Occupation—Joyce may work in a job with a higher accident rate or potential for occupational disease.

Educational Objective 8

8-1. Group insurance has these basic characteristics:
- Numerous individuals are insured under a master contract.
- Experience rating is used to determine premiums if the group is sufficiently large.
- Individual members are not normally required to provide evidence of insurability.
- The cost of group life insurance for covered employees is generally lower than individual coverage.

8-2. Underwriting factors considered for group life insurance include these:
- The group must be formed for a purpose other than purchasing insurance.
- The group should have a low turnover of individuals.
- Larger groups are more desirable than smaller groups.
- The group should have minimum participation requirements.
- Additional factors are also considered, such as efficient administration, prior loss experience of the group, age and sex composition of the group, and occupational hazards in the industry.

8-3. Group life insurance has these eligibility requirements:
- The employee generally must work full time but can occasionally work part time.
- A new employee must satisfy a probationary period before participating in the plan.
- A new employee must sign up for the insurance either before or during his or her eligibility period (generally thirty-one days).
- The new employee must be actively at work before the coverage becomes effective.

8-4. a. Peggy would not be required to pay anything for this coverage. Peggy's employer would pay the entire premium for the noncontributory plan of group term life insurance.

b. If Peggy quits her job, she has the right to convert the group term life insurance to an individual policy within thirty-one days.

Educational Objective 9

9-1. Because term life insurance policies typically do not develop cash values, purchasing a term life insurance policy would not help Catherine save money to put her son through college.

9-2. Based on the parent's modest income, he would be better served purchasing term life insurance. This is because he might be substantially underinsured if he purchased an ordinary life policy because its premiums are generally higher than term insurance until the insured reaches a certain age.

9-3. Because John lied on his life insurance application and because the two-year contestable period did not expire, his insurer has a right to contest the policy's validity.

9-4. The entire $300,000 face value is payable from the policy. Reba and her family might have elected to use the catastrophic illness rider to collect part of the face amount of the insurance to cover expenses while she was ill. The face value of the policy (or what remains if the catastrophic illness rider was used) will be paid to the beneficiaries over a period of ten years.

Direct Your Learning

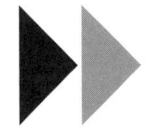

Assignment 12

Health and Disability Insurance

Educational Objectives

After learning the content of this assignment, you should be able to:

1. Describe major healthcare problems in the United States.
2. Describe types of private health insurance providers.
3. Describe the benefits provided by basic medical expense coverage.
4. Describe the basic types and characteristics of major medical insurance.
5. Describe important provisions that apply to most group health insurance policies.
6. Describe the types of plans and typical cost control provisions of dental insurance.
7. Describe the typical benefits provided by and eligibility provisions required for long-term care insurance.
8. Describe the characteristics of managed care plans.
9. Describe the distinguishing features of each of the following types of disability income insurance:
   - Individual disability income insurance
   - Group disability income plans
   - Social Security disability income benefits
10. Describe each of the following government programs for providing healthcare benefits:
    - Medicare
    - Medicare + Choice
    - Medicaid
    - Workers compensation

Study Materials

Required Reading:
- Personal Insurance
  - Chapter 12

Study Aids:
- SMART Online Practice Exams
- SMART Study Aids
  - Review Notes and Flash Cards—Assignment 12

Outline

- **Healthcare Problems in the United States**
  - A. Rising Healthcare Expenditures
  - B. Inadequate Access to Medical Care
  - C. Uneven Quality of Medical Care
  - D. Considerable Waste, Inefficiency, and Fraud
- **Providers of Private Health Insurance**
  - A. Commercial Insurers
  - B. Blue Cross and Blue Shield Plans
  - C. Self-Insured Plans
- **Basic Medical Expense Coverages**
  - A. Hospital Expense Insurance
  - B. Surgical Expense Insurance
  - C. Physicians' Visits Insurance
  - D. Additional Benefits
- **Major Medical Insurance**
  - A. Types of Major Medical Plans
  - B. Basic Characteristics
    1. Broad Coverage
    2. High Lifetime Limits
    3. Deductible
    4. Coinsurance Provision
    5. Exclusions and Internal Limits
- **Important Group Health Insurance Provisions**
  - A. Preexisting Conditions
  - B. Continuation of Group Health Insurance
  - C. Coordination-of-Benefits Provision
- **Dental Insurance**
  - A. Types of Group Dental Plans
  - B. Cost Controls
- **Long-Term Care Insurance**
  - A. Benefits Provided
  - B. Elimination Period
  - C. Eligibility for Benefits
  - D. Protection Against Inflation
  - E. Guaranteed Renewability
  - F. Cost
- **Managed Care Plans**
  - A. Health Maintenance Organization
  - B. Preferred Provider Organization
  - C. Exclusive Provider Organization
  - D. Point-of-Service Plan
  - E. Advantages of Managed Care Plans
  - F. Disadvantages of Managed Care Plans
- **Disability Income Insurance**
  - A. Individual Disability Income Insurance
    1. Limit on Amount of Disability Income
    2. Definition of Total Disability
    3. Residual Disability
    4. Elimination Period
    5. Benefit Period
    6. Renewability of the Policy
    7. Waiver of Premium
    8. Optional Disability Income Benefits
  - B. Group Disability Income Insurance
    1. Short-Term Plans
    2. Long-Term Plans
  - C. Social Security Disability Income Benefits
    1. Eligibility Requirements
    2. Benefits
- **Government Health Insurance and Healthcare Programs**
  - A. Medicare
    1. Hospital Insurance (Part A)
    2. Supplementary Medical Insurance (Part B)
    3. Financing Medicare
    4. Medicare + Choice
    5. Medigap Insurance
  - B. Medicaid
  - C. Workers Compensation
    1. Eligibility Requirements
    2. Workers Compensation Benefits
- **Summary**

For each assignment, you should define or describe each of the Key Words and Phrases and answer each of the Review and Application Questions.

Educational Objective 1
Describe major healthcare problems in the United States.

Review Questions

1-1. What are some of the problems currently facing the U.S. healthcare system?

1-2. Identify factors that explain the rise in healthcare spending.

1-3. Provide three examples of inadequate access to care by certain groups.

Application Question

1-4. Dr. Jones is a general practitioner. In his clinic he installed equipment that measures bone density as a diagnostic tool for osteoporosis. The equipment has been a great benefit. However, Dr. Jones now finds that he is in a quandary regarding the patients who are tested using the equipment. In the past, he would have ordered a bone density test for his patients over the age of fifty. Now, he is conducting tests for patients over the age of forty. He has changed his practice because some individuals between the ages of forty and fifty do begin to have thinning bones. If he should miss properly diagnosing such a patient when the equipment is readily available, he could be sued for malpractice. The average cost of an examination for his patients has increased because of the increasing frequency of bone density exams that are required. How does this scenario demonstrate healthcare problems in the United States?

Educational Objective 2
Describe types of private health insurance providers.

Review Questions

2-1. Briefly describe three types of private health insurance providers.

2-2. Describe a third-party administrator (TPA) contract as it relates to a self-insured plan.

2-3. What are some advantages of self-insurance to employers?

Application Question

2-4. Catherine is the human resources manager of a large commercial firm. She is encouraging her company to change from a commercial insurance healthcare plan to a self-insured plan. What benefits of this plan might Catherine's company expect from such a switch?

Educational Objective 3
Describe the benefits provided by basic medical expense coverage.

Key Words and Phrases

Basic medical expense coverages

Hospital expense insurance

Surgical expense insurance

Usual, reasonable, and customary (URC)

Physicians' visits insurance

Review Questions

3-1. Identify and describe three basic medical expense insurance coverages.

3-2. Explain how insurers determine reasonable and customary fees.

3-3. Identify six additional benefits often covered by basic medical plans.

Application Question

3-4. John and Barbara and their three children are insured under a comprehensive major medical expense plan that has a $100 calendar-year deductible with a $200 family deductible per calendar year. The plan also contains a common accident provision. An 80 percent coinsurance provision applies to eligible expenses over the deductible. There is also a stop-loss provision of $1,500, not including the deductible amount.

   a. John was hospitalized and incurred $2,400 of covered medical expenses. What dollar amount of these expenses would John be required to pay? Show your calculations.

   b. The following year, Barbara and her son, Pete, were injured in a boating accident for which their major medical expense plan provided coverage. Barbara's covered medical expenses were $1,200 and Pete's were $1,000. What total dollar amount would the family be required to pay toward these medical expenses? Show your calculations. (Ignore any contribution that might be available from other sources.)

   c. What is the maximum dollar amount that the family would have to pay toward covered medical expenses for all family members during any one calendar year?

Educational Objective 4

Describe the basic types and characteristics of major medical insurance.

Key Words and Phrases

Major medical insurance

Calendar-year deductible

Corridor deductible

Coinsurance

Stop-loss provision

Review Questions

4-1. Identify and briefly describe the two basic types of major medical insurance plans.

4-2. Describe the deductible provision of major medical insurance plans.

4-3. Identify common exclusions not covered under major medical plans.

Application Question

4-4. Karen and Sonya were comparing the major medical insurance coverages that they receive from their different employers. The plans both provided high limits of broad coverage. However, Karen's plan has an annual $200 deductible before the plan will pay expenses. Sonya's plan has no annual deductible, but her plan will pay only 80 percent of her losses for the first $1,000 of medical expenses each year. Explain why Karen's and Sonya's medical plans differ.

Educational Objective 5
Describe important provisions that apply to most group health insurance policies.

Key Words and Phrases

Preexisting conditions clause

Portability

Coordination-of-benefits provision

Review Questions

5-1. Explain whether preexisting conditions can be covered by group health insurance.

5-2. Describe the protection offered by the Health Insurance Portability and Accountability Act.

5-3. Under what conditions does the Consolidated Omnibus Budget Reconciliation Act of 1985 (COBRA) require employers to make health insurance available for the unemployed?

Application Question

5-4. Dwight enrolled in his company's group health insurance program so that his wife, Margaret, would be able to have surgery on the varicose veins in her legs. Margaret has taken medication for her condition for several years, but the problem has become more severe and her doctor recommended surgery. However, the hospital advised that the insurance company had denied coverage for the surgery. Considering the important group health insurance provision, why might the insurance company have denied coverage?

Educational Objective 6
Describe the types of plans and typical cost control provisions of dental insurance.

Review Questions

6-1. Identify and describe the two major types of dental insurance.

6-2. Explain how these dental insurance plan provisions help control costs:

　　a. New employees

　　b. Adverse selection

　　c. Exclusions

6-3. Explain how the predetermination-of-benefits provision works.

Application Question

6-4. The Evans family is insured under a nonscheduled dental insurance plan that includes a $50 annual deductible per person. The policy also includes an 80 percent coinsurance provision.

  a. Other than expenses for routine dental care, what types of expenses are likely to be covered by the Evans family's dental insurance plan?

  b. Explain how the Evans family will participate in the cost of dental care covered by this plan.

Educational Objective 7
Describe the typical benefits provided by and eligibility provisions required for long-term care insurance.

Key Words and Phrases
Long-term care insurance

Elimination period

Review Questions

7-1. Describe the benefits typically provided by long-term care insurance.

7-2. Describe the conditions under which a gatekeeper provision in long-term care insurance determines eligibility of benefits.

7-3. Describe two methods in which insurers protect the real value of long-term care insurance against inflation.

Application Question

7-4. Ray's father, Alfred, is ninety-six years old and no longer able to perform daily tasks to take care of himself. Although it is a difficult decision, Ray has placed Alfred in a nursing home. Ray purchased a long-term care policy for Alfred ten years ago. The policy has daily benefits of $120 for four years and an elimination period of 180 days. Describe the benefits that Ray should expect from the long-term care policy.

Educational Objective 8
Describe the characteristics of managed care plans.

Key Words and Phrases

Managed care

Health maintenance organization (HMO)

Preferred provider organization (PPO)

Exclusive provider organization (EPO)

Point-of-service (POS) plan

Review Questions

8-1. Explain the role of the primary care physician in an HMO.

8-2. Describe one advantage and one disadvantage of point-of-service plans.

8-3. Identify three advantages and three disadvantages of managed care plans.

Application Question

8-4. The XYZ Insurance Company provides coverage throughout the U.S. to policyholders. To service the claims for these policies, XYZ has 150 small claim offices distributed nationwide. Some of these offices include several claim representatives and support staff. Other offices consist of a single claim representative working from home. XYZ is making a choice between various types of managed care plans. They want a plan that will meet the needs of the claim representatives and their staff members. Evaluate the various managed care plans and their ability to meet the coverage needs of these employees.

Educational Objective 9

Describe the distinguishing features of each of the following types of disability income insurance:

- Individual disability income insurance
- Group disability income plans
- Social Security disability income benefits

Key Words and Phrases

Disability income insurance

Guaranteed renewable policy

Noncancelable policy

Conditionally renewable policy

Review Questions

9-1. Why are disability income insurance payments designed to replace only a part of a disabled worker's lost income?

9-2. What definitions of "total disability" are used most frequently in disability insurance policies?

9-3. Identify and describe the two categories of group disability income plans.

9-4. a. What requirements must be met to be eligible for disability income benefits under the Social Security program?

b. How is disability defined in the Social Security program?

c. Briefly describe the disability benefits under the Social Security program.

Application Question

9-5. Debbie is insured by a disability income insurance policy that is guaranteed renewable. Phil's disability income policy is noncancelable. Compare these two policies with respect to the insurer's ability to increase the premium.

Educational Objective 10
Describe each of the following government programs for providing healthcare benefits:

- **Medicare**
- **Medicare + Choice**
- **Medicaid**
- **Workers compensation**

Key Words and Phrases

Medicare

Medicare + Choice

Medicaid

Review Questions

10-1. a. Identify and briefly describe the benefits under Hospital Insurance (Part A) of the Medicare program.

b. Identify the benefits under Supplementary Medical Insurance (Part B) of the Medicare program.

c. What options are available under Medicare + Choice Part C of the Medicare program?

d. How is Medicare financed?

10-2. Briefly describe each of these:

a. Medigap insurance

b. Medicaid

10-3. Workers compensation laws are designed to provide benefits to workers who become disabled as a result of a job-related accident or disease.

a. What is the fundamental principle on which workers compensation is based?

b. What four basic benefits are provided under a typical workers compensation law?

Application Question

10-4. Jim is a forty-year-old self-employed auto mechanic. For ten years he's owned a shop specializing in repair and maintenance of European import luxury vehicles. Jim was severely injured in an automobile accident unrelated to his business. He has lost the use of his legs and has limited use of one hand. Describe the government health insurance that Jim might be entitled to and the benefits he could expect to receive.

Answers to Assignment 12 Questions

NOTE: These answers are provided to give students a basic understanding of acceptable types of responses. They often are not the only valid answers and are not intended to provide an exhaustive response to the questions.

Educational Objective 1

1-1. Some problems currently facing the U.S. healthcare system include:
- Rising healthcare expenditures
- Inadequate access to medical care (uninsured, rural, or welfare recipients)
- Uneven quality of medical care (by geographic location or by physician specialty)
- Considerable waste, inefficiency, and fraud (excess paperwork, nonstandardized forms, or abuse)

1-2. Some factors that explain the rise in healthcare spending include new and expensive medical technology; population growth that increases the demand for medical care, general price inflation; increased spending under Medicare and Medicaid and cost shifting by these programs to private insurers; aging of the population; and state-mandated private health insurance benefits.

1-3. Three examples of inadequate access to care by certain groups include:
- Millions of Americans (groups such as single adults under the age of twenty-five and low-income families) are uninsured and have no private or public health insurance.
- People in rural areas often have inadequate access to healthcare because of the shortage of physicians in many small rural communities.
- Welfare recipients have experienced problems finding physicians who will treat them promptly because of inadequate reimbursement rates.

1-4. This scenario illustrates healthcare problems in the U.S. by showing:
- The cost of heathcare is rising. In this case the new technology used by Dr. Jones is adding to the cost of examinations for his patients.
- Because many physicians are sued for medical malpractice, Dr. Jones is practicing defensive medicine by ordering procedures to avoid lawsuits.

Educational Objective 2

2-1. Three private health insurance providers include these:
- Commercial insurers—For-profit insurers provide individual and group health insurance coverage for medical expenses.
- Blue Cross and Blue Shield plans—Nonprofit plans provide coverage for hospital expenses, physician and surgeon fees, and related medical expenses and can offer coverage for major medical expenses.
- Self-insured plans—Employers provide health insurance benefits to their employees by paying part or all of the employee's health claim costs.

2-2. A third-party administrator (TPA) contract, when used as part of a self-insured plan, is an arrangement by which an insurer or another independent organization receives a fee for handling certain administrative details, such as enrollment of employees, recordkeeping, and claim payments.

2-3. Self-insurance has several advantages to employers:
- Health insurance costs might be reduced or might increase less rapidly because of the savings in state premium taxes, commissions, and the insurer's profit.
- Cash flow can be improved. The employer retains part or all of the funds needed to pay claims and earns interest on the money until the claims are paid.
- Self-insured plans are usually exempt from state laws that require insured plans to offer certain mandated benefits.

2-4. The benefits of a self-insured plan compared to a commercial insurance plan are that health insurance costs might be reduced because of savings in state premium taxes and commissions, and the insurer's profit. Cash flow might also be improved as the employer retains part of the funds needed to pay claims and earns interest on the money until the claims are paid. Self-insured plans are usually exempt from state laws that require mandated benefits.

Educational Objective 3

3-1. Three basic medical expense insurance coverages include these:
- Hospital expense insurance—Pays for covered medical expenses while the patient is in the hospital (daily room and board, drugs, laboratory fees, use of operating room, and X-rays).
- Surgical expense insurance—Pays part or all of a physician's fee for a surgical operation.
- Physicians' visits insurance—Pays for nonsurgical care provided by an attending physician other than a surgeon.

3-2. Insurers consider a fee to be reasonable and customary if it does not exceed the ninetieth percentile for the same medical procedure performed by other physicians in the same geographic area.

3-3. Six additional benefits often covered by basic medical plans include:
- Outpatient surgery when surgery is performed in a hospital or an office but the patient recovers at home
- Preadmission testing when diagnostic tests are given as an outpatient before admission to the hospital
- Diagnostic X-ray and laboratory expenses
- Home healthcare services by health professionals
- Extended-care facility services
- Hospice care

3-4. a. According to the comprehensive major medical expense plan that John and Barbara have, John would be required to pay $560, calculated:
$2,400 − $100 = $2,300.
$2,300 × 0.20 = $460.
John would be required to pay $100 (deductible) + $460 (coinsurance) = $560.

b. Because the common accident provision applies, the deductible for this accident is only $100.

$1,200 + $1,000 = $2,200.

$2,200 − $100 = $2,100.

$2,100 × 0.20 = $420.

The family would be required to pay $100 (deductible) + $420 (coinsurance) = $520.

c. The family deductible amount is $200. In addition, there is a stop-loss limit of $1,500 on expenses above the deductible.

$200 + $1,500 = $1,700.

The maximum the family would have to pay for covered medical expenses in one year is $1,700.

Educational Objective 4

4-1. Two basic types of major medical insurance plans include these:
- Supplemental medical insurance plan—Coverage for all medical expenses exceeding the limits of the underlying basic medical expense policy (sometimes also offers coverage for certain medical expenses not covered by the basic policy)
- Comprehensive medical insurance plan—Medical and expense coverages and major medical insurance in one policy

4-2. The deductible provision of major medical insurance plans specifies the amount the insured must pay before major medical insurance applies. (Generally, a calendar-year deductible is used for comprehensive plans and, for supplemental plans, a corridor deductible is used.)

4-3. Common exclusions not covered under major medical plans include eyeglasses and hearing aids, elective cosmetic surgery, experimental surgery, expenses covered by workers' compensation laws, expenses in excess of usual and customary charges, and services furnished by governmental agencies unless the patient has an obligation to pay.

4-4. Karen's plan has a calendar-year deductible. Once the deductible is satisfied each year, the insurer will pay for covered medical expenses. Sonya's plan includes a coinsurance provision, which also acts as a type of deductible. After Sonya meets her coinsurance payments for the first $1,000 of medical expenses, the insurer will pay for covered medical expenses. For yearly medical expenses under $1,000, Sonya will pay less out-of-pocket than Karen. If expenses exceed $1,000, both Karen and Sonya will be responsible for $200 of those expenses.

Educational Objective 5

5-1. Group health insurance covers preexisting conditions after the waiting period expires.

5-2. The Health Insurance Portability and Accountability Act restricts the right of employers and insurers to exclude or limit coverage for preexisting conditions. For example:
- This law guarantees that most workers who change jobs or lose jobs will have access to health insurance coverage.

- This law prohibits employers and insurers that offer health insurance plans from dropping people from coverage because they are sick or from imposing waiting periods for preexisting conditions for more than twelve months (eighteen months for late enrollees).
- This law requires employers and health insurers to give credit for previous coverage so that workers who maintain continuous health insurance coverage (without a gap of sixty-three days) can never be excluded because of a preexisting condition.

5-3. The Consolidated Omnibus Budget Reconciliation Act of 1985 (COBRA) requires employers to make health insurance available for workers who quit their jobs, are laid off, or are fired. The COBRA law applies to employers of twenty of more employees. Under COBRA, employees and covered dependents can elect to remain in the employer's plan for a limited period after a qualifying event occurs (such as termination of employment for any reason except gross misconduct, death of the employee, divorce, etc.) that results in the loss of coverage. Insureds who elect to remain in the group plan can be required to pay up to 102 percent of the group rate.

5-4. Margaret has a preexisting condition. Employer-sponsored group health insurance plans are prohibited from excluding or limiting coverage for a preexisting condition for more than twelve or eighteen months for a medical condition that is diagnosed or treated during the six months before the enrollment date in the plan.

Educational Objective 6

6-1. The two major types of group dental insurance include these:
- Scheduled dental plan—Covered dental services are listed in a schedule, and a specific dollar amount is paid for each service. (The patient pays the difference between the dental plan benefit payment and the dentist's charges.)
- Nonscheduled dental plan—Dentists are reimbursed for most dental services on the basis of their usual, reasonable, and customary charges subject to limitations in the plan. (The patient usually pays an annual deductible and coinsurance requirement.)

6-2. a. Provisions for new employees help control dental costs by making new employees meet a waiting period before certain dental expenses are covered, such as twelve months for orthodontia.
b. Adverse selection provisions help control dental costs by requiring employees desiring coverage after their eligibility period expires to meet a waiting period, such as one or two years. Otherwise, they might have reduced benefits.
c. Exclusions, such as cosmetic dental work, lost or duplicate dentures, and expenses covered by workers' compensation, also help control dental costs.

6-3. Most dental plans contain a predetermination-of-benefits provision. If the estimated cost of treatment exceeds a certain amount, such as $200, the dentist submits to the insurer a plan of treatment, which specifies the services needed. The insurer then determines the amount the plan will pay. If the amount to be paid is lower than the estimated cost of treatment, the patient can seek less costly care.

6-4. a. Other than expenses for oral examinations and cleaning, the Evans family's dental insurance plan will likely cover these types of expenses:
- Fillings
- X-rays
- Orthodontia
- Extractions
- Dentures

b. The Evans family will probably participate in the cost of dental care covered by this non-scheduled dental insurance plan by paying the family's first $50 or so of dental expenses each year (deductible) and 20 percent of any additional expenses (coinsurance). However, diagnostic and preventive services are not always subject to this deductible or coinsurance requirement, and some services, such as orthodontia, might be reimbursed at a lower percentage.

Educational Objective 7

7-1. Long-term care insurance typically provides cash benefits for these:
- Skilled nursing home care—Medical care provided by skilled medical personnel twenty-four hours a day under the supervision of a physician (care by registered nurses or physical therapists)
- Intermediate nursing care—Care for a stable condition that requires daily care but not twenty-four-hour nursing supervision
- Custodial care—Care to assist the patient in the activities of daily living (assistance for dressing, bathing, eating, and using the toilet)

7-2. A gatekeeper provision in long-term care insurance states the requirements that the insured must meet to receive benefits. A common type of gatekeeper provision requires that the insured be unable to perform a certain number of activities of daily living (ADLs), such as eating, bathing, walking, dressing, maintaining continence, etc. Benefits can be paid if the insured cannot perform a certain number of ADLs (such as two out of five) without help from another person.

7-3. Two methods in which insurers protect the real value of long-term care insurance against inflation are:
- Some plans allow insureds to purchase additional amounts of insurance in the future with no evidence of insurability. The premium is based on the insured's current age, but evidence of insurability is not required.
- Some plans provide for an automatic benefit increase in which the daily benefit is increased by a specified percentage for a number of years, such as 5 percent annually for the next ten or twenty years.

7-4. The elimination period is 180 days, assuming that Alfred has not received care or previously entered a nursing home. Coverage will not begin until Alfred has received care for that length of time. Following the elimination period, the insurer will pay up to $120 per day for four years.

Educational Objective 8

8-1. The primary care physician in an HMO is the "gatekeeper physician" who determines whether the patient should be referred to a specialist.

8-2. Point-of-service plans have the major advantage of preserving freedom of choice for plan members by making it possible to see a physician or specialist of their choice. However, a major disadvantage is the higher out-of-pocket cost that the member must pay.

8-3. Three advantages of managed care plans are:
- Healthcare costs can be held down because these plans emphasize cost controls.
- Plan members often pay little or no out-of-pocket costs for covered medical services.
- Managed care plans provide many loss-prevention services, such as routine physical examinations, Pap smears, immunizations, well-child care, and eye examinations.

Three disadvantages of managed care plans are:
- The emphasis on cost control might reduce the quality of care provided to some patients.
- Managed care plans often provide a financial incentive, such as a bonus to network physicians, to hold down costs.
- Some HMO physicians are not free to treat patients without restrictions. For example, plan physicians might be required to obtain approval from plan administrators before certain tests and procedures are given.

8-4. Various managed care plans offer these characteristics:
- An HMO provides comprehensive care, but the employees must choose healthcare providers who are part of the network. Because an HMO operates in a limited geographic area, this would not meet the needs of all of the employees.
- A PPO contracts with healthcare providers to provide medical services at discounted fees. The employees would not be required to receive treatment from a preferred provider, but they would have a financial incentive to do so. A PPO might be a good plan for XYZ's employees.
- An EPO is like a PPO that does not pay for medical care outside of the network of preferred providers. This would not be effective for the employees.
- A POS has a network of preferred providers that provide care at reduced costs out-of-pocket. If care is received outside the network, the care is covered, but the employees will pay a higher coinsurance charge and deductible. A POS might be a good plan for XYZ's employees.

Educational Objective 9

9-1. Disability income insurance payments are designed to replace only a part of a disabled worker's lost income because:
- The disabled worker may pay no taxes, or fewer taxes, on the disability income.
- The disabled worker may extend the period of disability and postpone the return to work if these payments provide a high disability income.

9-2. Definitions of "total disability" used most frequently in disability insurance policies include these:
- The insured is unable to perform the major duties of his or her own occupation.
- The insured is unable to perform the duties of any gainful occupation for which he or she is reasonably suited by education, training, and experience.
- For an initial period, the insured is unable to perform the major duties of his or her own occupation. After the initial period expires, the insured is unable to perform the duties of any gainful occupation for which he or she is reasonably suited by education, training, and experience.
- The insured loses the sight of both eyes, or the use of both hands, both feet, or one hand and one foot (presumptive total disability).

9-3. The two categories of group disability income plans include these:
- Short-term plans—Require a short elimination period and pay lower disability income benefits to eligible workers for a relatively short time for nonoccupational disabilities.
- Long-term plans—Require a long elimination period (three to six months) and pay higher disability income benefits to eligible workers for a relatively long time for both occupational and nonoccupational disabilities.

9-4. a. Disabled workers must meet eligibility requirements to receive disability income benefits under the Social Security program:
- Earn a certain number of credits (quarters of coverage) for work in covered employment.
- Satisfy a five-month waiting period.
- Meet the stated definition of disability.

b. The Social Security program defines "disability" as having a physical or mental condition that prevents doing any substantial gainful work, and the condition must be expected to last at least twelve months or to result in death.

c. The Social Security program provides disability benefits to these people:
- Disabled beneficiaries who meet the eligibility requirements
- Unmarried children under age eighteen
- Unmarried children age eighteen or older who became disabled before age twenty-two and are eligible for benefits based on the disabled worker's earnings
- A spouse at any age who is caring for a child under age sixteen (or a child who became disabled before age twenty-two)
- A spouse age sixty-two or older even if he or she is not caring for children

9-5. Both Debbie's guaranteed renewable disability income insurance policy and Phil's noncancelable disability income insurance policy cannot be canceled after they are issued. For Phil's policy, the insurer guarantees renewal to some stated age and also guarantees that the premium will stay the same. For Debbie's policy, however, the insurer guarantees renewal to some stated age but does not guarantee the premium—it can increase.

Educational Objective 10

10-1. a. Hospital Insurance (Part A) of the Medicare program provides these benefits:
- Inpatient hospital care—Inpatient coverage for up to ninety days for each benefit period
- Skilled nursing facility care—Inpatient coverage for the patient requiring skilled nursing care (after at least three days of hospitalization)
- Home healthcare services—Coverage for home healthcare, medical supplies, and medical equipment in the home if the patient requires skilled care for an injury or illness (with or without previous hospitalization)
- Hospice care—Coverage for hospice care (but not curative treatment) if a physician certifies that the patient is terminally ill and the hospice is certified by Medicare
- Blood transfusions—Coverage for the cost of blood transfusions furnished by a hospital or skilled nursing facility during a covered stay (except for the first three pints of blood)
- Additional benefits—Coverage for mammograms, Pap smears, pelvic examinations, breast examinations, diabetes glucose monitoring, diabetes education, bone mass measurements, and colorectal and prostate cancer screening

b. The Supplementary Medical Insurance (Part B) of the Medicare program provides these benefits:
- Physicians' services in the hospital, the office, or elsewhere
- Medical supplies and durable medical equipment
- Clinical laboratory services (blood tests and urinalyses)
- Home healthcare visits if the beneficiary is not covered by Part A
- Outpatient hospital services for the diagnosis or treatment of illness or injury
- Blood (except for the first three pints of blood)
- Ambulatory surgical services

c. Medicare + Choice Part C of the Medicare program provides these options:
- Original Medicare plan
- Original Medicare plan with supplemental policy
- Medicare managed care plan
- Private fee-for-service plan

d. Medicare Part A is financed by a payroll tax on earned income of all U.S. workers. The employee and employer pay the same Medicare tax rate, and the self-employed pay a tax rate that is double the employer rate. Medicare Part B is financed largely by a monthly premium paid by insured persons and by general revenues of the federal government.

10-2. a. Medigap insurance—Private health insurance that pays part or all of the covered medical expenses not paid by Medicare.

b. Medicaid—A federal-state welfare program that covers the medical expenses of low-income persons, including those who are aged, blind, or disabled; members of families with dependent children; and certain children and pregnant women.

10-3. a. Workers compensation is based on the liability-without-fault principle. Employers are held absolutely liable for job-related injuries or disease incurred by their workers, regardless of fault.

b. Following are four basic benefits of a typical workers compensation law:
- Medical expenses—Paid in full without deductibles or coinsurance
- Weekly disability income benefits—Paid to disabled workers after a short elimination period (typically three to seven days)
- Death benefits—Paid if the worker dies from a job-related accident or disease
- Rehabilitation services and vocational retraining—Paid to restore disabled workers to productive employment

10-4. Assuming that Jim has been entitled to Social Security disability benefits for twenty-four months and is considered disabled, he is entitled to Medicare disability benefits.
- Under part A of the program, Jim may receive inpatient hospital care, nursing facility care, and home healthcare service.
- Under part B he might also receive physicians' fees, outpatient hospital services, and related medical services.

s.m.a.r.t. tips — When you take the randomized full practice exams in the SMART Online Practice Exams product, you are using the same software you will use when you take the national exam. Take advantage of your time and learn the features of the software now.

Exam Information

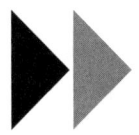

About Institute Exams

Exam questions are based on the educational objectives stated in the course guide. The exam is designed to measure whether you have met those educational objectives. The exam does not test every educational objective. Instead, it tests over a balanced sample of educational objectives.

How to Pass Institute Exams

What can you do to make sure you pass an Institute exam? Students who successfully pass Institute exams do the following:

- Use the assigned study materials. Focus your study on the educational objectives presented at the beginning of each course guide assignment. Thoroughly read the textbook and any other assigned materials, and then complete the course guide exercises. Choose a study method that best suits your needs; for example, participate in a traditional class, online class, or informal study group; or study on your own. Use the Institutes' SMART Study Aids (if available) for practice and review. If this course has an associated SMART Online Practice Exams product, you will find an access code on the inside back cover of this course guide. This access code allows you to print (in PDF format) a full practice exam and to take additional online practice exams that will simulate an actual national exam.

- Become familiar with the types of test questions. The practice exam in this course guide or in the SMART Online Practice Exams product, will help you understand the different types of questions you will encounter on the exam.

- Maximize your test-taking time. Successful students use the sample exam in the course guide or in the SMART Online Practice Exams product to practice pacing themselves. Learning how to manage your time during the exam ensures that you will complete all of the test questions in the time allotted.

Types of Exam Questions

The Correct-Answer Type

In this type of question, the question stem is followed by four responses, one of which is absolutely correct. Select the *correct* answer.

> Which one of the following persons evaluates requests for insurance and determines which applicants are accepted and which are rejected?
> a. The premium auditor
> b. The loss control representative
> c. The underwriter
> d. The risk manager

The Best-Answer Type

In this type of question, the question stem is followed by four responses, only one of which is best, given the statement made or facts provided in the stem. Select the *best* answer.

> Several people within an insurer might be involved in determining whether an applicant for insurance is accepted. Which one of the following is primarily responsible for determining whether an applicant for insurance is accepted?
> a. The loss control representative
> b. The customer service representative
> c. The underwriter
> d. The premium auditor

The Incomplete-Statement or Sentence-Completion Type

In this type of question, the last part of the question stem consists of a portion of a statement rather than a direct question. Select the phrase that *correctly* or *best* completes the sentence.

> Residual market plans designed for individuals who have been unable to obtain insurance on their property in the voluntary market are called
> a. VIN plans.
> b. Self-insured retention plans.
> c. Premium discount plans.
> d. FAIR plans.

"All of the Above" Type

In this type of question, only one of the first three answers could be correct, or all three might be correct, in which case the best answer would be "All of the above." Read all the answers and select the *best* answer.

When a large commercial insured's policy is up for renewal, which of the following is (are) likely to provide input to the renewal decision process?
a. The underwriter
b. The loss control representative
c. The producer
d. All of the above

"All of the following, EXCEPT:" Type

In this type of question, responses include three correct answers and one answer that is incorrect or is clearly the least correct. Select the *incorrect* or *least correct* answer.

All of the following adjust insurance claims, EXCEPT:
a. Insurer claim representatives
b. Premium auditors
c. Producers
d. Independent adjusters